Volume 4 / Issue #1

EDITORIALIZING ... **2**
Guest editorial by *Monster!* publisher Brian Harris!

COVER REVIEW | Hammer's FRANKENSTEIN ... **8**
Louis Paul stitches together the tale of Hammer's Victor Frankenstein and his monsters!

DRACULA ACCORDING TO HAMMER ... **24**
Troy Howarth chronicles Hammer Studios' devotion to the Eternal Bloodsucker!

REVIEWS | Monster Movies from Around the World! ... **39**
SNOWBEAST, SPOOKIES, SOULKEEPER, and more!

MY FIRST TIME ... **59**
Monster! authors recount their earliest encounters.

IT *AIN'T* LEGEND: MANGLING MATHESON ... **64**
Steve Bissette covers the adaptations of Richard Matheson's monumental novel of the last man on earth: *I Am Legend*.

DINOSAURS ATTACK! ... **81**
John Harrison discusses the classic Topps cards

THE HOUSE OF RAMSAY, PART 8 ... **91**
Review of the autumn years Ramsay film **GHUTAN**!

MONSTER #13 Movie Checklist ... **95**

Front cover: Creature as blockhead from **THE EVIL OF FRANKENSTEIN**
Back cover: Rip-roarin' Italian poster for the same film (art unsigned)

Contributors: Eric Messina, Stephen R. Bissette, Steve Fenton, Louis Paul, John Harrison, Brian & India Harris, Troy Howarth, Greg Goodsell, Christos Mouroukis, Mike T. Lyddon, and Tim Paxton.

Timothy Paxton, Editor & Design Demon
Steve Fenton, Editor & Info-wrangler
Tony Strauss, Edit-fiend • Brian Harris, El Publisher de Grand Poobah

MONSTER! is published monthly. Subscriptions are *not* available.
© 2014 WK Books, unless otherwise noted. All rights reserved. No part of this publication may be reproduced, distributed, or transmitted in any form or by any means, including photocopying, recording, or other electronic or mechanical methods, without the prior written permission of the publisher, except in the case of brief quotations embodied in critical reviews and certain other noncommercial uses permitted by copyright law. For permission requests, write to the publisher: "Attention: Permissions Coordinator," at: Tim Paxton, Saucerman Site Studios, 26 W. Vine St., Oberlin, OH 44074 • kronoscope@oberlin.net

MONSTER! contains photos, drawings, and illustrations included for the purpose of criticism and documentation. All pictures copyrighted by respective authors, production companies, and/or copyright holders.

Editorializing

Guest editorial by MONSTER! publisher Brian Harris!

WANTED! More Readers like Brian and India Harris!

Has Wildside-Kronos really made it to 2015? Time flies when you're doing something you truly love. It seems like just yesterday Tim and I released (then rereleased) *Weng's Chop* #0, not knowing whether the endeavor would fall flat on its face and we'd be heading back to our respective lives with thoughts of what could have been. Instead we persevered, pushed, pimped, banged heads on walls, pencils on paper, fingers on keyboards, and allowed our enthusiasm to inspire those around us. We re-launched *Monster!*, brought in two amazing editors (Tony Strauss and Steven Fenton), surrounded ourselves with passionate writers and electrifying illustrators and we wrote about the things we loved. 22 issues of both *Monster!* and *Weng's Chop*, soon to be 23, and we're closing on 10,000 copies sold. It seems we're onto something.

So, here's my promise to you, the reader: We not only plan to continue sharing our love for monsters, but with each and every issue sold we're going to push the very limits of our abilities as well. When you purchase a Wildside-Kronos publication, you'll know every single penny spent was worth it.

Now that all of that is out of the way, I've decided to take Tim's suggestion and interview my 4-year-old daughter India, to find out what she thought about one of my favorite films, **THE WAR OF THE GARGANTUAS** (フランケンシュタインの怪獣 サンダ対ガイラ [1966]; see *Monster!* #12). She and I just watched it the other day, and, while it's still fresh in her little spongy brain, it's best to get her thoughts on it...

Brian: Hey India, how are you doing today?

India: I'm doing good. Doing really good.

Brian: So you and I got to watch WAR OF THE GARGANTUAS **a day or so ago. Did you like it?**

India: Yes. I liked the fighting Gargantua. I liked the fighting ones. I liked the green one and the brown one.

Brian: Which Gargantua did you like the most?

India: I liked the green scary one. He was scary and crazy, just like I am when I get candy. And what are those two—these things, what are they?

Brian: Those are buttons in Daddy's writing program. Back to WAR OF THE GARGANTUAS: **Who did you think would win?**

India: I think the brown one. He's really taller and he's browner.

Brian: Did you think the movie was scary?

India: No, I was brave. Are you typing in, "No, I was brave"?

Brian: Yup.

India: Could I type it in?

Brian: Sure you can.

India: Yuihgyyuj-poihltlmbvm.jgvfyudcxssz.

Brian: Good job!

India: Thanks. I like to type all the time. Kmgyuk-k;lkikiop;';o0p988ugvt

Brian: Do you like watching Godzilla or WAR OF THE GARGANTUAS **more?**

India: Godzilla.yyy.lmnb+

Brian: **Would you like Daddy to find you a WAR OF THE GARGANTUAS toy?**

India: Uh, no. Or yes. But I want them to be big. This big, as big as my ponies. Five foot tall. Twenty-four foot tall.

Brian: Did you know the monsters were named SANDA and GAIRA?

India: Ghkjuy. Yes.

Brian: Do you think those are good names? What would you rather call them?

India: I would call the brown one SAIRADAIRA and the green one KAOSDADAOS. Now can I type?

Brian: *Good names!* **Thank you for the awesome interview, little girl. Would you watch another monster movie with me soon?**

India: Sure. Yes. Yes sir.uuuuufffklpuyypoukhnbtfrdeeol90=plhhgrhyyy

~ Brian & India Harris

The Ghosts of The Frankensteins
The Past, Present, & Future of What Could Have and Should Have Been

Second Editorial

Kiwi Kingston and Katy Wild in a scene from Hammer Films' **THE EVIL OF FRANKENSTEIN**

Monster! has been around, in one form or another, since 1988, and over the past twenty-odd years I have been told that I have written some apparently amusing stuff. If that is true, then you may be aware that I have a particular fondness for Frankenstein's creature in film and in literature. Considering that both the creator and the creature (alternately called Frankenstein) have made around a hundred-plus appearances in film and TV (from cameos to full-on starring roles). Only a few of these roles have ever treated the monster in a way that I found at all proper...or interesting in the least. When I penned a previous editorial (back in *Monster!* #6), there was discussion on how inherently wrong the monster was in Fred Dekker's 1987 film **THE MONSTER SQUAD**. Rather than addressing the creature for what he was in Shelley's book—both intelligent and articulate—Tom Noonan's monster was a lovable blockhead with stunted cognitive skills. That is *not* what I want in a film about Shelley's monster, no matter how cute he is with the kids in the film. If you want my take on the least offensive variations on the theme, then maybe I will get off my butt and finally write that comprehensive article on Frankenstein Cinema. (I have notes on the project. Somewhere. In a box. Maybe in my attic crawlspace? Who knows...)

The cover for this issue is one I Photoshopped from a commonly seen production still for **THE EVIL OF FRANKENSTEIN** (see p.17), Hammer Films' third in their popular take on the doctor and his monsters, and a film that is often panned by critics. Yes, monster*s*, in the plural, since Hammer

3

What should have been the logical sequel to **THE GHOST OF FRANKENSTEIN**? Well, a cool mash-up wherein the Monster with his new brain (that of the cunning Ygor) plans the destruction of London because, well, he's a jerk. It's up to Sherlock Holmes to put a stop to the monster

was smart enough to feature an "all-new" creature in each and every film, more-or-less side-stepping the deadly game of sequel arcing that framed *most* of Universal's *Frankenstein* run (from 1931-1948). Now, I adore most all of the Universal films (except for **FRANKENSTEIN MEETS THE WOLF MAN** [1943], which was a terrible letdown for me as a kid), despite their treatment of the monster and its development—or lack thereof—post-**THE BRIDE OF FRANKENSTEIN** (1935). There has been so much written about the first three films that something like **THE GHOST OF FRANKENSTEIN** (1942) has been left to flail about in a critical no man's land, not unlike Hammer's **EVIL**, which was a critical disappointment for many. I beg to differ, and I will go into this briefly here, saving any longer, better analysis of both films for a later issue.

For me it is less the execution of the films themselves than the ideas that were worked into them. These ideas—or even only inklings of them—are something more powerful for me than the actual productions.

I have two major concerns when it comes to Frankenstein films: their treatment of the creature and the manner in which Frankenstein's lab is portrayed. First and foremost in importance for me is how the creature and its intelligence is treated. I personally prefer to have the creature portrayed as the intelligent sentient being it was in Shelley's novel. And what's wrong with that? Granted, it would mean adding more words to a script and possibly more character development, and maybe the actor cast in the role would

have to really muster some skills and sharpen their chops. Karloff's monster was just on the verge of this important aspect, as he shared his love of cigars and music and struggled with stringing words together into simple sentences in Universal Studios' aforementioned **THE BRIDE OF FRANKENSTEIN**. Then of course that development was snuffed-out and abandoned when the monster next appeared in **THE SON OF FRANKENSTEIN** (1939), with its inability to speak never being really explained other than—*maybe*—brain damage was the cause of it. That muteness was cured in **THE GHOST OF FRANKENSTEIN**, wherein the villainous hunchback Ygor voluntarily has his brain inserted into the body of the monster. In my opinion, the result was quite possibly the best thing that could *ever* have happened to the Universal series! Imagine the grey matter of the highly intelligent, cunning—and *evil*—Ygor inside his noggin atop the indestructible body of the hulking horror of The Monster. Such a formidable villain could have taken the film industry by storm! Just thinking about the potential of this once again takes my breathe away. Back in the day I had written a short treatment called "Sherlock Holmes and the Monster of London Tower".[1] As the title

---

[1] I must admit I was influenced by two "continuing adventures of the Frankenstein Monster" novels by Robert J. Myers: *The Cross of Frankenstein* (1975) and *The Slave of Frankenstein* (1976), wherein the insidiously intelligent creature was still wreaking further havoc on mankind. These were two books that I read as a teen, and I imagined that they would be great if adapted as films. *Slave* had three great hooks for my 14-year-old brain: not only was the creature smart and articulate, *but* Oberlin, Ohio (my home town) was mentioned as well as the involvement of John Brown (a distant relative of our family), the white American abolitionist who conspired

suggests, Holmes was pitted against the hybrid horror of The Monster/Ygor, who happens to be up to no good. Nothing short of world domination was its goal. But this was not going to happen at Universal, and the promise of a viciously smart monster was squashed when it was resurrected in the lackluster **FRANKENSTEIN MEETS THE WOLF MAN**. In that film, the monster (cleverly played by Bela Lugosi, who was Ygor in both **SON** and **GHOST**) was rendered both mute and dumb (as in mindless) after spending years in suspended animation within a block of ice. Such a disappointment! I would have loved to have had the creature, fully energized by the crazy Dr. Mannering (Patric Knowles), wax eloquently about how he was going to first tear the wolfman limb from limb then run off to terrorize mankind...with the intrepid Sherlock Holmes hot on his trail. But, nope. That kind of fun was never going to happen in the1940s Hollywood machine. Bummer. By the end of **FMTWM** the monster fell again by meeting yet another demise, only to return the following year in the above-cited **HOUSE OF FRANKENSTEIN, HOUSE OF DRACULA** (1945), and—weirdly—in **ABBOTT AND COSTELLO MEET FRANKENSTEIN** (1948) as a lumbering lump played by Glenn Strange. (Ironically, only Mel Brooks' wacky parody **YOUNG FRANKENSTEIN** [1974] took the brain transplantation angle seriously—with classically comic results.)

Universal had a chance to take the series to another level. They could have stepped up their game after **GHOST**. But that was not to happen. It wasn't until more than a decade later that Hammer Studios' **THE CURSE OF FRANKENSTEIN** (see p.11) helped usher in the second era of the series. While the studio produced one of the screen's more igneous sociopaths with Peter Cushing's portrayal of the good Doctor Frankenstein, his monsters were not what was important. The creatures were more or less the ends to a means. We would get to thrill to Frankenstein puttering around with his wonderfully archaic devices and sewing together sloppy body parts more than we get to see the various creations do their thing. Only two of the monsters would really fit into my creature criteria: Karl/Creature from **THE REVENGE OF FRANKENSTEIN** ([see p.15] my all-time fave Hammer Frankenstein film) and Professor Richter/Creature from **FRANKENSTEIN MUST BE DESTROYED** (see p.20). You could add the odd Hans/Christina "transsexual Creature" from **FRANKENSTEIN CREATED WOMAN** (see p.18) to the list, but that's more about soul transference and not actually a piecemeal critter at all.

"I am ... Ygor!"

Rare French lobby still for
THE GHOST OF FRANKENSTEIN

---

with the creature for weapons and rebellion...*and* there were vivid sex scenes with the monster and a few young ladies, too!

[Note: For more about the Hammer series, see Louis Paul's article following this editorial.]

Other brainy variations showed up in films like Calvin Floyd's **VICTOR FRANKENSTEIN** (a.k.a. **TERROR OF FRANKENSTEIN**, 1977, Sweden/Ireland), Kevin Connor's Slovakian/American/German TV miniseries **FRANKENSTEIN** (2004) and the recent teleseries *Penny Dreadful* (2014, USA/Ireland/UK). In these three fine examples, the creature was not Hollywood's hoary flat-top lunk, but instead appeared much closer to the description in Shelley's book:

"His limbs were in proportion, and I had selected his features as beautiful. Beautiful! Great God! His yellow skin scarcely covered the work of muscles and arteries beneath; his hair was of a lustrous black, and flowing; his teeth of a pearly whiteness; but these luxuriances only formed a more horrid contrast with his watery eyes, that seemed almost of the same colour as the dun-white sockets in which they were set, his shrivelled complexion and straight black lips".

So why did I feature the creature from **THE EVIL OF FRANKENSTEIN** on the cover of this issue? After Chris Lee's turn in **CURSE**, Kiwi Kingston's lumbering lummox is the most brainless of Victor Frankenstein's creations. It is also my favorite Frankenstein monster after the pathetic Hans/Creature and all-to-brief Richter/Creature. **EVIL** is without a doubt the most pulpy of the Hammer *Frankenstein* franchise. The first thirty minutes are, for me, some of the best of the series, with the essential bits being the Baron recalling how he came about creating a monster, studying it once it was alive, and then watching as it fell to its death in a glacier after a police officer put a bullet in its brain. Here we have a monster whose likeness is that of a block of flesh which Frankenstein chopped and sewed together with no second thought of the thing's resultant ugliness (a brilliantly disturbing makeup job

---

From Shelley's description of the creature, one would think she was channeling current Goth culture. The creature's classic look—long black hair, pale skin, and blackened lips—rarely showed up in any dramatization of the book. The few instances when it did appear include:- **Top:** Luke Goss as the monster in Kevin Connor's 2004 TV miniseries. **Center:** Rory Kinnear as the Creature in Frankenstein's lab from *Penny Dreadful* (2014); note the bank of Leyden jars behind hm. **Left:** Per Oscarsson in **VICTOR FRANKENSTEIN** (1977), sporting some serious black lipstick!

by Roy Ashton and Phil Leakey). As per his sociopathic leanings, Frankenstein only brought this monstrous thing to life *because he could*. He cared little for treating it like a human being, keeping it in a corner of the lab on a mat of straw, never addressing it in any fashion, observing and taking notes as it wanders around the lab and feeds on raw meat. Frankenstein remains aloof and detached from it, without having any social interaction whatsoever with the creature beyond the aforementioned feeding and clothing of it (had this been real life, I doubt that the "good" doctor would have supplied his creation with a stitch of clothing). It was a science fair project, that's all. This part of the film *rocked*! But so far as I am concerned, the rest of **EVIL** is mere puttering around with the plot, as Frankenstein discovers his monster frozen in the glacier. He revives it, and, with the help of a local hypnotist, he is able to restore the monster to its full strength once more. But, as always, the doctor's plans soon go off the track again when the monster runs amok, thanks to the malicious mesmerist and his thirst for vengeance.

Onto the second of my criteria: specifically, the lab wherein the monster is made. Sure, Universal had all the fancy loud machinery that threw flashy lighting all over the place, but it was those rinky-dink and ultimately more realistic "do-it-yourself" labs that inhabited Hammer Studios which I ultimately fell in love with. Here are glass aquariums full of eyeballs, hands and hearts (etc.), arms attached to beakers and tubes attached to bare wires powered by some really wonderfully created wooden and metal apparatuses that, despite looking like crap at times, would no doubt have efficiently produced sufficient power for Frankenstein's needs. Forget those dumb "electric eels" which were used in Kenneth Branagh's 1994 "reboot" **MARY SHELLEY'S FRANKENSTEIN** (which nonetheless does have its moments) and were mentioned in the seriously shitty **I, FRANKENSTEIN** (2014, D: Stuart Beattie) to power the monster's—to quote Zacherle—"internal workin's"; I want to see stacks of multiple Leyden jars (as in some of the films and in Frankenstein's lab seen in *Penny Dreadful*), as well as a huge Faraday disk (*à la* **CURSE**), and even a primitive wood-and-copper dynamo like that seen in **EVIL** warms my tinkerer's soul. That's my kinda monster-maker gear!

So, what was this ranting all about? Uh, *nothing*, really, other than the reason why I put the repulsively delightful blockheaded mug of the monster from **THE EVIL OF FRANKENSTEIN** on this issue's cover. That's all. Seems like good enough of an excuse as any.

~Tim Paxton

Old School Technology: Peter Cushing as Victor Frankenstein at the Faraday disk generator from **THE CURSE OF FRANKENSTEIN**

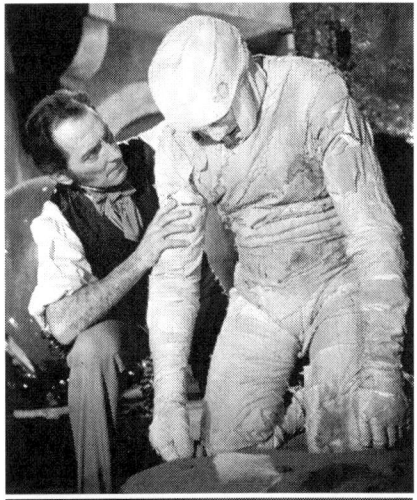

Top: Cushing as Victor Frankenstein examines his newly reborn science project (Kiwi Kingston). **Above:** Classic shot of Kingston as the creature, sporting grotesque makeup by Roy Ashton and Phil Leakey. Both stills are from **THE EVIL OF FRANKENSTEIN** (see also p.17)

COVER REVIEW

Louis Paul's
CREATURE FEATURES
HAMMER FILMS' GOTHIC TALES OF HORROR:
THE FRANKENSTEIN SERIES

by Louis Paul

Nearly forgotten by a whole new age of writers who grew up in the 'Eighties and beyond, the movies produced by the British film studio Hammer Films were a varied bunch. After a few slow starts, they finally found their footing in the late 1950s by resurrecting (in full-color) popular horror film characters of the past: Dracula, Dr. Frankenstein, and more. As the years passed, and society became more permissive, heavy amounts of blood and naked female skin began to appear in the movies they produced in the 'Seventies. By the time of their sad demise in 1979, Hammer Films' output was reduced to Hammer House of Horror *(1980)*, an uneven television series with tales of mystery and horror (produced and shown in the UK), and an odd number of cinematic failures (the ill-timed vampire/kung fun mash-up **THE LEGEND OF THE 7 GOLDEN VAMPIRES** [七金屍 / Qi jin shi, a.k.a. **THE SEVEN BROTHERS MEET DRACULA**, 1974, UK/Hong Kong; see p. 36], and **THE LADY VANISHES** *[1979, UK]* remake being the more obvious ones).

Hammer has been revived in recent years, but their output has been slow, and a bit uneven. Matt Reeves' **LET ME IN** *(2010, UK/USA)*, the remake—in English—of Tomas Alfredson's popular and well-received Swedish film **LET THE RIGHT ONE IN** (Låt den rätte komma in, *2008*) garnered good reviews, but it was made much too soon after the original and comparisons were just in, noting that the remake was slightly inferior. Also in more recent years, two additional Hammer thrillers were produced (i.e., David Keating's **WAKE WOOD** *[2010, UK/Ireland]* and Antti Jokinen's **THE RESIDENT** *[2011, UK/USA]*), but they received scant theatrical release in the US before heading over to cable television and VOD. A successful throwback to their gothic period, James Watkins' **THE WOMAN IN BLACK** *(2012, UK/Canada/Sweden)*, starring Daniel "Harry Potter" Radcliffe, did improve the studio's new reputation and raised eyebrows for its qualities as a restrained, atmospheric ghost thriller. However, production slowed down again, and it took a few years for a follow-up to be made. Tom Harper's **THE WOMAN IN BLACK 2: ANGEL OF DEATH** is that film, and, by most accounts, it's not that good and has been stuck on the limbo shelf for months (it is due to receive a US release this very month).

In this issue of Monster! I will be discussing Hammer Films' Frankenstein series. All but one of the films starred Peter Cushing, but all will be covered here. Firstly, however, here's a history of Hammer...the film studio.

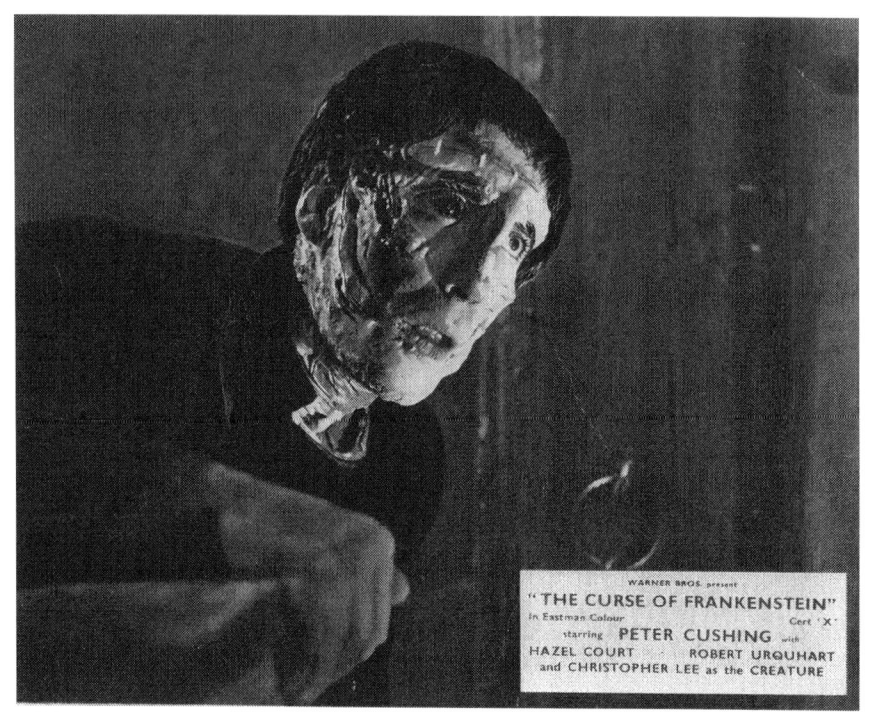

A Face Only A Mad Doctor Could Love: Managing to emote with conviction even through Phil Leakey's and Roy Ashton's for the time exceedingly gruesome makeup, Christopher Lee generates both horror and pathos as the manmade creature everybody loves to hate

Hammer was founded in 1934 by William Hinds (1887-1957), a businessman and amateur actor who named the company after his stage name: Will Hammer (itself cribbed from Hammersmith, the area of London where he lived). After forming Hammer Productions Ltd., filming began on a low-budget comedy-drama, **THE PUBLIC LIFE OF HENRY THE NINTH** (1935, UK), directed by Bernard Mainwaring. However, Hinds was quick to learn that producing movies meant that you needed a distributor to help get them into theaters. Enter Enrique Carreras, who owned a few movie theaters in the Blue Hall chain, and with Hinds, formed Exclusive Films, solely to distribute Hammer product.

Hammer's first films were an unusual lot:

Denison Clift's **THE MYSTERY OF THE MARIE CELESTE** (a.k.a. **PHANTOM SHIP**, 1935, UK) was a ghost thriller set at sea, featuring Bela Lugosi in a supporting role; and, the following year, J. Elder Wills'

SONG OF FREEDOM starred Paul Robeson as a dockworker who moonlights as an opera singer and becomes a singing sensation. Affected by the stirrings of a pre-War economy that was beginning to show signs of uneasiness, Hammer stopped making films, while Exclusive stayed in business—barely—by distributing low-budget fare produced by other companies, as well as product imported from the US.

World War II effectively dampened Hammer Films, but, when James Carreras (1910-1990), son of Enrique, and Anthony Hinds (1922-2013), son of William, assumed control of Exclusive after the war, they resurrected Hammer Films for the long haul. Seeking to provide postwar entertainment for the masses, they licensed popular pulp characters from radio, producing a number of titles that spotlighted a British naval officer who was also a two-fisted spy fighting enemy forces. The *Dick Barton* series was popular enough that it allowed Hammer to move into two spacious old houses outside of London, and these locations became not only their chief production studios, but were often seen onscreen over the years in a countless number of Hammer movies. The early 'Fifties saw production of a number of noirish thrillers, and also a thriller about Jack the Ripper (i.e., Godfrey Grayson's **ROOM TO LET** [1950, UK]). The next four years saw the production of numerous working class comedies (which were popular with postwar British audiences); as well as Seymour Friedman's **THE SAINT'S RETURN** (a.k.a. **THE SAINT'S GIRL FRIDAY**, 1953, UK), a movie featuring Leslie Charteris' popular Simon Templar character, alias "The Saint"; and Terence Fisher's **SPACEWAYS** (1953, UK), a low-budget science fiction thriller (this prior to Hammer acquiring the rights to produce film versions of popular early British television sci-fi serials which were initially televised live by the BBC then subsequently adapted as big screen remakes at Hammer). **THE QUATERMASS XPERIMENT** (a.k.a. **THE CREEPING UNKNOWN**, 1955), **X THE UNKNOWN** (1956), and **QUATERMASS 2** (a.k.a. **ENEMY FROM SPACE**, 1957, all UK [see *Monster!* #11 for coverage of these three films]) were all popular with theatrical audiences, and even received wide distribution outside of England too.

Towards the tail-end of the '50s, Hammer Films then set about reviving the ever-enduring characters of Dracula and Frankenstein, who were last seen in a series of uneven but wildly influential B&W films from Universal Studios in the US. Hammer's edge was that, while the Universal titles took place in the contemporary times of the 'Thirties and 'Forties, for the most part, the Hammer productions were drenched in the Victorian age melodramatics and romanticism present in the original source novels by Mary Wollstonecraft Shelley (1797-1851) and Bram Stoker (1847-1912), and amplified them to better suit more modern mores, adding in dollops of heaving bosoms, and—for the first time—*blood*...for these movies were shot in color! The rest of Hammer's history is well-documented elsewhere, so let's move on to their *Frankenstein* series…

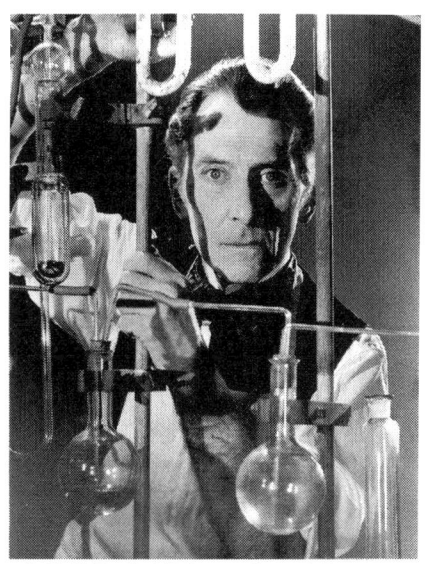

It Ain't Rocket Science: A specially-posed publicity portrait of Peter Cushing (1913-1994) as Baron Victor Frankenstein, in his element

THE CURSE OF FRANKENSTEIN

UK, 1957. D: Terence Fisher
Wr: Jimmy Sangster
S: Peter Cushing, Christopher Lee, Robert Urquhart, Hazel Court, Valerie Gaunt

In what most certainly had to be a shocking opener for its time, the movie begins with a disheveled, unshaven Baron Victor Frankenstein (Cushing) awaiting his execution in a cell as he recounts his life story to a priest whose sole purpose there is to hear his confession. Next we see a younger version of the Baron, who had inherited the family estate. The young Victor (Melvyn Hayes) hires one Paul Krempe (Urquhart) to be his tutor, and, as the years pass—and Hayes, the young actor playing the Baron, "turns into" Cushing—becomes his partner in scientific experimentation. Victor is obsessed with the writings of other scientists, and in particular, the theme of life after death.

Reviving a deceased dog only leads the now slightly unhinged and very obsessed Victor to greater heights…and he begins to plunder cemeteries for body parts in his quest to create a living person from the remains of the recently dead. Paul does not share Victor's obsessions, and this creates a rift between them. Things take a turn for the worse when a vacationing Paul returns to the Frankenstein castle to learn that Professor Bernstein (Paul Hardtmuth), the aged, distinguished

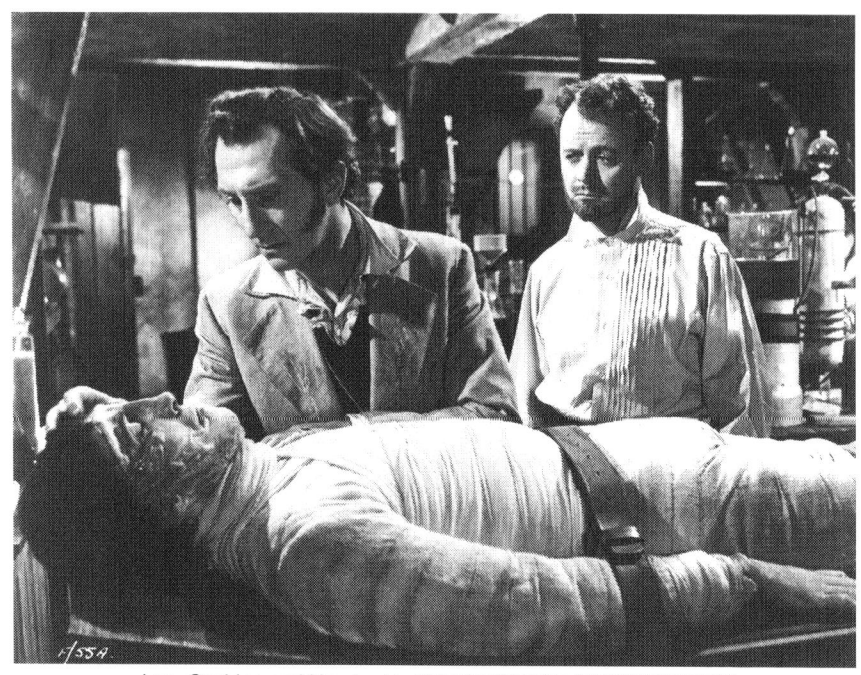

Lee, Cushing and Urquhart in **THE CURSE OF FRANKENSTEIN**

scientist who had been visiting, has since died. Victor had caused his death, and now wishes to implant his brilliant brain into the body that he has assembled piecemeal. Once Paul figures out that Victor was responsible for Bernstein's death, they have a physical altercation over the brain, and it becomes damaged. Nonetheless, it's still implanted into the head of the stitched-together being, who becomes a mute, raging-with-hatred...*monster* (Christopher Lee, in his breakout role). Once the creature breaks free of the castle and murders someone, they shoot it, and Paul leaves. However, the Baron has other plans, and we find that being shot in the head only makes the monster...even *more* psychotic!

The estate's full-bosomed maid, Justine (Gaunt), who "entertains" the Baron on the side when he's not dallying with his much more conservative fiancée, Elizabeth (Court), threatens him with blackmail after spying on him at his secret work and learning of the creature. Of course, the Baron shortly arranges it so that the monster attacks and murders the woman. Things go full-tilt when Paul is invited back by Elizabeth out of concern for Victor's mental health, only to learn that the Baron has not only revived the creature but has become obsessed with trying to correct its psychosis. Escaping once again, and threatening Elizabeth, the creature is set aflame and falls into acid, dissolving all evidence of its existence.

This takes us full-circle back to the beginning of the film, as it is noted that now is the time for the Baron's execution. It appears he had been accused of the maid's murder, and now that there is no proof of the creature that he created, no one believes him when he says it was responsible; not even Paul, who briefly visits him in his cell, will speak of the monster, preferring that Victor be executed for his crimes against man...and God.

Try to imagine being a horror movie buff in 1957, who had grown up with the black-and-white Universal horror movies starring Boris Karloff, Bela Lugosi, and Lon Chaney, Jr., and who had seen the numerous sequels, follow-ups, and similar films from other studios. Imagine if you can how the later Universal horror films featuring Frankenstein and the vampire Dracula edged ever closer towards camp as writers and directors battled with great difficulty to come up with novel, intriguing and entertaining stories. The series itself was certainly capped with a film intended as a comedic spoof but which contained enough intentionally horrific and macabre moments to make a fitting capper to many of the Universal horrors before it: namely, Charles T. Barton's **ABBOTT AND COSTELLO MEET FRANKENSTEIN** (1948, USA).

Hammer's "straight" film from a decade later was soaked in rich colors. The sets used were the same ones that the studio used for other films (as well as serving as their production offices). The cast, fine stage actors all, who had experience in supporting roles in films to that point, were a good match with their director, Terence Fisher (1904-1980). More than a mere journeyman technician, Fisher imbued nearly all of his work with subtextual details that rewarded repeat viewings. And then—in glorious Eastmancolor!—there's the heaving flesh-tone bosom of Valerie Gaunt. And, if your eyes didn't pop out at that sight, there's also the incredibly colorful makeup of Phil Leakey. Leakey was responsible for Chris Lee's creature; and it had to be different enough from the Jack Pierce-created design for the monster as interpreted by Boris Karloff for the Universal films, as they were notoriously difficult about allowing Hammer to recreate that look. As I have frequently noted elsewhere in other articles and reviews, the immensely popular horror films produced by Universal Studios in America began to pale by the end of the 1940s, replaced by the even more wildly popular Atom Age horrors of the nuclear bomb, and Cold War paranoia…and, of course, let's not forget giant insect monsters, crawling eyes, and homegrown psychopaths!

The British production house Hammer Films had much success with pre-WW2, and post-WW2 dramas, comedies, and even science fiction films, until the thought of making a Frankenstein film reached fruition.

In its preproduction infancy stages, **THE CURSE OF FRANKENSTEIN** would see Hammer originally partner with another company, Associated Artists Productions (AAP), which was run by Max J. Rosenberg (1914-2004) and Milton Subotsky (1921-1991), who would later co-create Hammer's rival in horror, Amicus Productions. Lore has it that Subotsky sent Hammer a script, patterned loosely on Rowland V. Lee's Universal monster classic **THE SON OF FRANKENSTEIN** (1939, USA), but it was rejected for fear of infringing on Universal's copyright. Jimmy Sangster was commissioned to rewrite the script into a workable production, and then the decision was made to film it in color. When brought to the British Board of Film Censors (BBFC) before production was started, the script, together with a production outline, received a stern response: "We are concerned about the flavor of this script, which, in its preoccupation with horror and gruesome detail, goes far beyond what we are accustomed to allow even for the 'X' [rating] category. I am afraid we can give no assurance that we should be able to pass a film based on this present script…"

Undeterred, Hammer went ahead and filmed it anyway, with little change—and the rest is history!

Instead of concentrating on the monster, as the majority of the Universal Frankenstein films had done, Hammer's take was making the film center more upon the doctor. In this version of Mary Shelley's classic novel *Frankenstein: or, The Modern Prometheus* (1818), now long in the public domain, Victor Frankenstein is the monster. Going against the laws of science and arrogant towards the communal thoughts of established catholic religion, he is obsessed with creating life; even if he has to traverse unnatural paths—up to and including seduction, deception, and murder— to achieve his final goal. With a heavy gothic feel, and utilizing sets that were actually redressed rooms from the core Hammer production home itself, the movie was the first horror film shot in color in England, with plentiful heaving full breasts encased in too-tight bodices clearly on view, and blood everywhere in the surgical laboratory…to the scarred creature itself. Horror films were never the same afterwards, and this movie really put Hammer on the map, so to speak, and they spent the next few decades making many sequels and a variety of other horror films, with the content

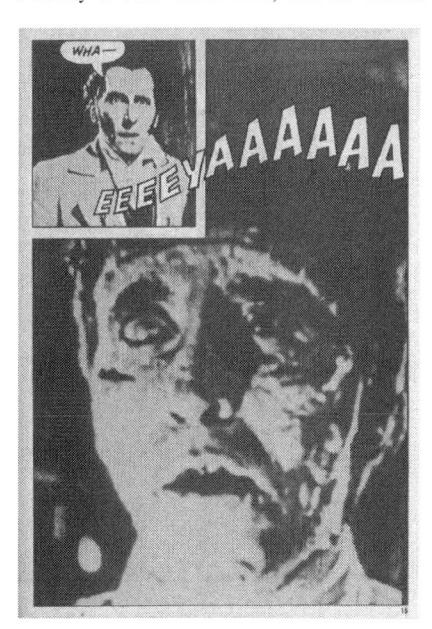

Page 15 of Warren Publishing's photo-comic magazine *Famous Films #2* (1964), showing still-frame images taken from **THE CURSE OF FRANKENSTEIN**. The same issue also included a photo-comic condensation of Hammer's **DRACULA** (under its US release title, **HORROR OF DRACULA** [see p.25])

Italian poster for **THE REVENGE OF FRANKENSTEIN** (art by Sandro Simeoni, who here signed his name as "Sym"; he later used the signature "Symeoni")

becoming more graphic (in terms of both sex and blood) as the 'Sixties and 'Seventies wore on.

Terence Fisher had directed an astounding 26 films in a ten-year period before he helmed this, the first color horror film ever made in England. *Monster!* readers might well recognize his name from such other genre-related films as **STOLEN FACE** (1952, UK), **FOUR SIDED TRIANGLE** and the aforementioned **SPACEWAYS** (both 1953, UK), three sci-fi dramas; and all of them were made for Hammer before they turned major profits with the *Quatermass* films. The five films he directed in the *Frankenstein* series enabled him to be experimental by combining undertones of religion, sensuality, and more. He didn't do too badly with the *Dracula* series films he directed, either: **DRACULA** (a.k.a. **HORROR OF DRACULA** [1958; see p.25]), **THE BRIDES OF DRACULA** (1960), and **DRACULA, PRINCE OF DARKNESS** (1965, all UK; see p.27). Fisher would occasionally work outside of the Hammer house of horror, usually for smaller independent companies, making sci-fi features, and even these—notably **ISLAND OF TERROR** (1966, UK)—bear distinct touches of the director's style. Fisher's last three films were for Hammer, including the revered, Dennis Wheatley-based occult adventure horror film

THE DEVIL RIDES OUT (a.k.a. **THE DEVIL'S BRIDE**, 1968, UK).

Peter Cushing (1913-1994) began his acting career on the stage (in a production of *Hamlet*), and appeared in minor roles in everything from James Whale's golden age film version of Alexandre Dumas' **THE MAN IN THE IRON MASK** (1939, USA), to the Laurel & Hardy movie, **A CHUMP AT OXFORD** (1940, UK), directed by Alfred J. Goulding. After being cast in Olivier's cinematic adaptation of **HAMLET** (1948, UK) in a major supporting role, fame of sorts followed for Cushing with an award-winning, powerful dramatic role as the protagonist of the BBC live production of George Orwell's **1984** (1954, UK). Various appearances in costume dramas and on the stage followed, until he was cast in the lead as Baron Victor Frankenstein for the present film. A major member of Hammer Films' in-house company of actors, he would go on to appear in a large number of their productions, and in those for other rival studios as well (including Amicus), and, in later years, those of American-International Pictures too. For his true gentlemanly nature, Cushing was informally dubbed "The Gentleman of Horror" by his peers and fans alike. Of all the films he appeared in, his performances as Dr. Frankenstein rank among his very best. In hindsight, his most notable appearance in a motion picture—one that has been seen by audiences too numerous to count—is that of the Grand Moff Tarkin in George Lucas' **STAR WARS** (1977, USA). Peter Cushing died of cancer in 1994 at age 81, and at least I have a memory that I will always cherish of meeting him in person at one of the very few *Famous Monsters of Filmland* Hammer Film conventions, held in New York City ten years before that.

Christopher Lee: What more can be said of this legendary actor—still actively working at 92!—who has had so many books written about him (including his own 1977 autobiography, *Tall, Dark and Gruesome*) as well as being subject of a number of documentaries? Like Cushing, Lee began his acting career on the stage, and within a short amount of time went from being a "spear-carrier" extra to having notable supporting roles in movies. True that the role of the "creature" in **THE CURSE OF FRANKENSTEIN**—Lee's only appearance in one of Hammer's *Frankenstein* series—is a nonspeaking one, but Hammer was confident enough in the actor that he landed the prime role of Count Dracula in their 1958 film, and he would make numerous appearances in Hammer sequels (as well as other movies) as Dracula over the coming decades. Trying to get away from the image of the bloodsucking vampire as which he had been typecast—much like Sean Connery was thought synonymous with the character of James Bond for decades, even after Roger Moore had replaced him in the 'Seventies—Lee embraced the Hammer films, and the Dracula character in later years, and because of the notoriety…he is still working…sixty-two years after his first notable performance as an actor.

THE REVENGE OF FRANKENSTEIN
UK, 1958. D: Terence Fisher
Wr: Jimmy Sangster
S: Peter Cushing, Francis Matthews, Eunice Gayson, Oscar Quitak, Michael Gwynn, Lionel Jeffries, Richard Wordsworth

In a prologue, we see that that the ending of the previous film (**CURSE**) was not what we thought, and that the Baron (Cushing) had somehow arranged for the body of the priest who had heard his final confession to be substituted for his own at the guillotine instead.

Years later, we find Dr. Victor "Stein" (Cushing; *who else?!*) practicing medicine in the town of Carlsbrück. Dr. Stein has wealthy patients, but appears to take more pride in attending to the poor and maimed, who cannot afford proper medical care. Assisting the doctor is Karl (Quitak), a kindly, deformed man. However, all this is really a smokescreen, as Dr. Stein is still very much obsessed with creating life from death, and Karl is his lab assistant. Karl has a "thing" for Margaret (Gayson), another of Dr. Stein's assistants; one with a pronounced bust…this *is* a Hammer film, after all! Also assisting with the treatment of the patients is Dr. Hans Kleve (Matthews), who is slowly let into Dr. Stein's confidence.

Stein transplants the brain of the dwarfish Karl into a new body (Gwynn), and the operation proves a success. However, Kleve notes that a previous experiment with apes had ended in tragedy and psychosis. The "new" Karl begins to exhibit dangerously violent behavior, and starts to show physical changes as well. Slowly, his body and face begins to contort, the paralytic arms and legs begin to hamper him, and it seems he is reverting to his former hunchbacked self. Karl even appears at Margaret's home and frightens her. After crashing a party, before collapsing Karl calls out to Stein and pleads with Dr. Frankenstein to help him. Kleve, who knows Stein's true identity, implores him to flee Carlsbrück before the authorities find out who he really is…but it's too late. Once the grave is exhumed, and they find the

British poster. Note the BBFC's "X" rating, which didn't mean the same thing in the UK as it later came to mean in the US

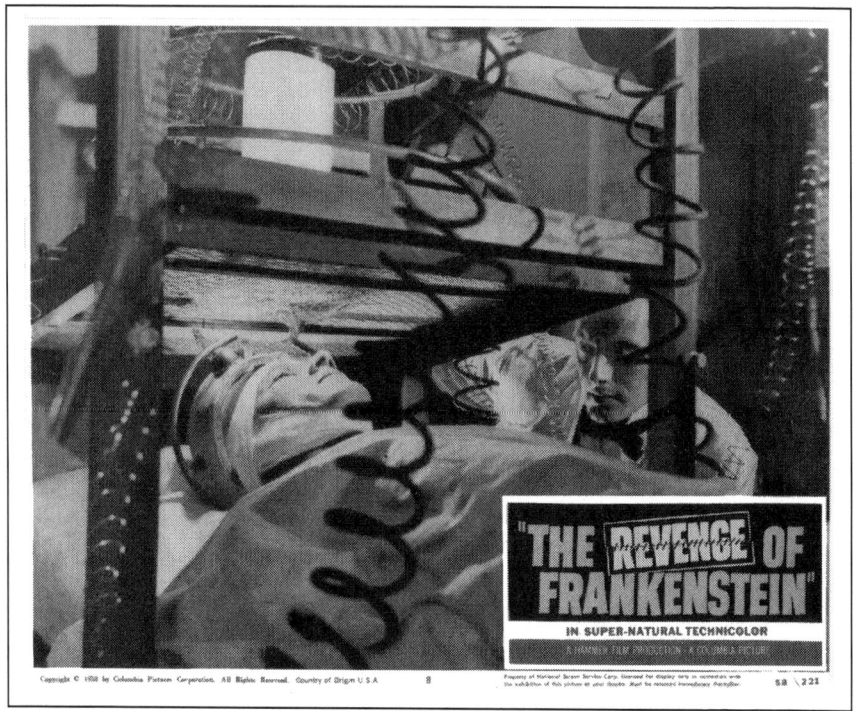

Michael Gwynn as the creature-in-progress and Francis Matthews as the lab assistant in a US lobby card for **REVENGE**

body of the priest, it's all over for Dr. Frankenstein. At around this time, word travels fast that the "kindly" Dr. Stein is in fact—*surprise, surprise!*—Frankenstein, and, frightened and angry that their amputated limbs may have been used in an experiment (or worse) and they've been treated by a madman, they wreak havoc on Stein's hospital. With shards of glass, wood and bricks they brutally attack Stein, and by the time Kleve finds his bloodied body there is barely time left to do anything to save it.

The film's dark coda features the mustached Dr. Franck (Cushing) attending to patients at another clinic in another German town. Apparently, Kleve was successful in transferring Frankenstein's brain to that of another corpse; one that looked startlingly similar to the doctor.

How does one follow-up a movie like **THE CURSE OF FRANKENSTEIN**, especially when the creature has been seemingly killed off, and our protagonist imprisoned and about to be executed? You make a very *different* kind of movie, that's how; and what was most successful about the first film is amplified and accentuated here. Clearly, Peter Cushing's portrayal of Dr. Frankenstein showed that *he* himself was the monster. Much more of a psychological drama imbued with moments of terror, **REVENGE** is a fine sequel, with moments of great pathos. We see Dr. Stein treating the poor patients and feel empathy for them, and maybe newfound respect for him—until later, when we discover that he may be using their discarded body parts ("That leg has to come off!") for his own use. Francis Matthews provides good support as the handsome assistant, but I could never get over the fact that if I closed my eyes, it sounded like Cary Grant was assisting Peter Cushing! Matthews' vocal tonations were that close to Grant, whom he grew up with, and was his roommate. Eunice Grayson (who would later make more memorable appearances as Sylvia in a couple Connery-era Bond movies, including Terence Young's **DR. NO** [1962, UK]) is the eye candy on view, but there's little time for sex in this movie as it concentrates instead on the dogged determination of Dr. Frankenstein to resume his experiments. Things take a mighty macabre turn for the finale, which I'm sure must have been truly startling to '50s audiences.

A different kind of horror movie, and a worthy successor to the first in the series.

16

THE EVIL OF FRANKENSTEIN

UK, 1964. D: Freddie Francis
Wr: John Elder
S: Peter Cushing, Sandor Elès, Peter Woodthorpe, Kiwi Kingston, Duncan Lamont, Katy Wild

Breaking continuity with the previous film (**REVENGE**), our crazy protagonist (Cushing) has resumed calling himself Dr. Frankenstein once more, and has returned to Switzerland, to his home in Karlstaad, where the events of **CURSE** took place. It seems that the doctor seeks to locate—and if possible, revive—the creature from the first film (therein played by Christopher Lee). He does indeed locate the monster, and it's frozen solid in a block of ice. What becomes immediately apparent is that the "new" monster no longer resembles Lee's version in Phil Leakey's makeup at all; and now, since they had worked out a distribution deal with Universal Pictures, Hammer were allowed to use a makeup design—by their own artist, Roy Ashton—similar to that done by Jack Pierce on Boris Karloff (and Lugosi, Chaney, Jr. and Glenn Strange). Here, the monster (XL former wrestler Kingston) appears to be damaged, but Frankenstein and his assistant, Hans (Elès) take the body to see if they can revive the creature. Meanwhile, Zoltan (Woodthorpe), a local charlatan who practices hypnosis among other things in a local circus, is contacted by Frankenstein in the hopes that maybe hypnotherapy will save the damaged and diseased mind of the monster. (If you recall, or if you don't…in the first film in Hammer's series, the brain was originally that of a revered famous scientist but it got damaged, and further so, when the monster was shot in the head while it was on a rampage.) Zoltan is a hard-drinking, lecherous creep who immediately sees that he can control the monster for his own gain: i.e., the murder of police authorities who gave him a hard time…as well as the kidnapping of a shapely beggar girl (Wild) for his own sexual amusements. However, the huge, hulking monster is more primal than ever, and controlling it is what Zoltan wants to do, to the point of having the monster steal gold for him. Fortunately, Dr. Frankenstein, who has been uncharacteristically benign thus far, shows signs of the insidious Baron of old, and not only is Zoltan dispensed with, but the creature dies in a fiery ending.

Terence Fisher was busy with postproduction on another film for Hammer (**THE GORGON** [1964, UK]), and also in '64 was into preproduction for his impending science fiction feature **THE EARTH DIES SCREAMING**, financed by American "cheapie" producer Robert L. Lippert for the UK branch of his company. So, due to Fisher's unavailability, Freddie Francis, a cinematographer of some note, directed the present film instead. He would be the chief cameraman on a number of interesting and varied flicks, like Jack Cardiff's **SONS AND LOVERS** (1960, UK), for which Francis won an Academy Award, as well as Jack Clayton's **THE INNOCENTS** (1961, USA/UK), both David Lynch's **THE ELEPHANT MAN** (1980, USA/UK) and **DUNE** (1984, USA), and even the Scorsese/De Niro remake of **CAPE FEAR** (1991, USA). As a director, Francis' work is uneven, and stays chiefly within the British horror genre: Besides **EVIL**, he also helmed the multi-story shocker **DR. TERROR'S HOUSE**

Peter Cushing hits the "On" button in **THE EVIL OF FRANKENSTEIN**. The creature waiting to be born was played by Kiwi Kingston

Kiwi Kingston as the patchwork creature and Katy Wild as the feral woman get cozy in a classic "monster gets the gal" scene

OF HORRORS (1964), THE SKULL (1965), TORTURE GARDEN (1968), DRACULA HAS RISEN FROM THE GRAVE (1968; his best Hammer film [see p. 29]), the hilarious TROG (1970), CRAZE (1974 [see *Weng's Chop* #6.5]), plus the still-influential omnibus film TALES FROM THE CRYPT for Amicus in 1972.

Peter Cushing's Dr. Frankenstein takes a backseat to the scene-stealing ham of Woodthorpe's shady mesmerist, Zoltan. Woodthorpe (1931-2004) was a busy character actor on the stage and screen for decades, and herein, for some reason, director Francis appears more interested in the machinations of the actor's Zoltan character. Only midway through the film do we see Dr. Frankenstein reasserting himself and challenging Zoltan, who has not only hypnotized the other man's monster for his own use, but also attempts to dominate Frankenstein too…a *fatal* mistake!

A majority of critics and viewers (myself included) disliked this entry in Hammer's *Frankenstein* series upon its release, and the intervening years have only been slightly more kind to it. I've always felt that Ashton's makeup seems more like some child's failed experiment with *papier mâché* rather than a clever "reimagining" of the makeup worn by Chris Lee in CURSE. I've met people who really enjoy this movie, and, while it's not bad entertainment, it pales when placed alongside other films in this series, especially the following movie…

FRANKENSTEIN CREATED WOMAN
UK, 1967. D: Terence Fisher
Wr: John Elder (Anthony Hinds)
S: Peter Cushing, Susan Denberg, Thorley Walters, Robert Morris

Prologue: A man is taken to his death by the authorities. He is to be beheaded. Taunted by the assembled onlookers, he sees his young son Hans among them, watching. The man protests that his son should not be witnessing his execution, and as a priest approaches, the boy runs off. However, he hides as he watches the blade slide down and then…*blackness*.

It's now ten years or more later, and Hans has since grown into a handsome young man (Morris), who assists Dr. Frankenstein (yes, Cushing again!) and the elder Dr. Hertz (Walters) in their new experiments. Having failed in taking the brain of one man from one body and inserting it into another one—although it had obviously worked for the doctor, as can be seen at the end of REVENGE—Frankenstein now hopes to transfer souls from a recently deceased person to another cadaver that he plans to revive, in the hopes that he can restore life to the dead. You have to give a good mad scientist credit, as he's always thinking up new variations on his own failed experiments!

It develops that Hans has a major crush on Christina (Denberg), the daughter of a local innkeeper. Most of the left side of her body is paralyzed and she has a partially disfigured face. But Christina is a humble and kind woman who is often the target of humiliation at the hands of rich young scoundrels who frequent the inn. In a subtextual context, you can feel that three of these men in particular would like nothing better than to gang-rape the unfortunate woman and possibly even kill her afterwards, as their taunts have an air of true degeneracy about them.

Getting into a fight with these creeps, Hans is beaten, but manages to get a good slash into one of his attackers. They return later that night, and murder Christina's father. The accused winds up being Hans (who is innocent, of course), simply because he was the son of a convicted and executed killer himself. Poor Hans is beheaded, but Frankenstein and Hertz quickly grab his still-warm head, planning to trap his soul for later revivification. Meanwhile, distraught over the death of her father, the taunts of the rich kids and the death of Hans, who she secretly loved, Christina drowns herself in despair. The villagers bring her lifeless body to Dr. Frankenstein, and he comes up with an idea: although it is too late to save Christina since she took her own life, it may be possible to transfer Hans' soul into her body…

Success awaits, and a busty, statuesque Christina results! Having been cured of all her physical deformities and paralysis, she is now a real stunner, with the mind and soul of her dead lover inhabiting her mind and body. Fortunately, Christina has little to no memory of her past. Frankenstein and Hertz tutor her, and teach her to be the beautiful woman that she now is. But slowly, virtually subliminal thoughts enter her mind that she must kill the three men responsible for the deaths of Hans, herself, and her father. After first seducing and then murdering the trio one by one, Christina then drowns herself once more, since she has nothing left to live for. Frankenstein simply walks away from the scene; probably his greatest and most difficult medical triumph to date has simply ended her own life.

Fisher returns to direct a film in the *Frankenstein* series, and it is immeasurably better than the previous movie (**EVIL**). Anthony Hinds was the son of the Hammer studio's cofounder, and often wrote scripts under the pseudonym John Elder. Certainly, I consider this as one of the finest British horror films of all time. Fisher's dabbling in science fiction-themed movies and thrillers at the time appears to have influenced his newfound interest in psychological terror and psychosexual themes. For the majority of the movie, Cushing's performance as Dr. Frankenstein is more nuanced than you will find anywhere in the series. Still determined and obsessed, he is almost paternal towards Christina as he realizes he must become a surrogate father figure to her once he has to assist her newfound rebirth into the world.

Susan Denberg is eye candy, for sure! A statuesque Austrian-German model and actress, this was her only co-starring film role. After being a *Playboy* "Playmate of the Month" in '66, she also appeared on the "Mudd's Women" episode of television's *Star Trek* (1966-69, USA). Apparently, embroiled in drug abuse scandals, she subsequently returned to her native Austria.

Thorley Walters (1913-1991) was an actor who excelled at playing the role of the older, often dotty English gent. With the aid of a little makeup, he could easily become the elder gentleman, the kindly grandfather or the befuddled drunkard (a role he would perform in a number of Britcoms, both of the big screen and small screen variety).

Poster for the 1968 Italian release of **FRANKENSTEIN CREATED WOMAN** (art unsigned)

FRANKENSTEIN MUST BE DESTROYED

UK, 1969. D: Terence Fisher
Wr: Bert Batt, Anthony Hinds
S: Peter Cushing, Simon Ward, Veronica Carlson, Freddie Jones, George Pravda

While previous entries in this series depicted the doctor Baron Victor von Frankenstein (Cushing) as seductive, arrogant, cunning, charming—if not always in that order—in this film he is a totally irredeemable character who has a singular vision and literally revels in terrorizing others so that he can attain the ultimate goal of creating life after death…*sort of.*

Knowing that he needs assistance, Frankenstein seeks out Dr. Karl Horst (Ward), and his lover Anna (Carlson), who runs a boardinghouse. Amounting to a first for the series, when Anna refuses to participate, Frankenstein actually physically assaults and rapes her! The doctor's plan this time is to abduct a brilliant brain surgeon named Brandt (Pravda) from an asylum—he's gone *crazy*, of course!—in order to transplant his brain into that of another physician, one Professor Richter (Jones). This time Frankenstein has it all planned out, with little to no chance for any deviation from his plans, to create a perfect being with the brain of a once-intelligent and revered surgeon in the body of a skilled physician. But Frankenstein's clouded vision—he needs Brandt's skills at brain transplants to aid with his own experiments—doesn't allow for how he will cure the madness that has set in in his patient. Once they have kidnapped both victims and transplanted the brain of one person into another, all hell breaks loose as Brandt becomes confused, and a bit addled, as he's not been cured of his madness. Seeking solace in the arms of his wife, Brandt (or rather, his brain in the body of Richter) unwittingly frightens her, and, realizing that Frankenstein has turned him into a monster—a man with a damaged brain in the body of another man—he seeks vengeance. The fiery climax sees Brandt/Richter carrying the body of Frankenstein into a raging fire that he has set, as retribution for the wrongs done to him.

Unlike any Hammer horror film before it, **FRANKENSTEIN MUST BE DESTROYED** takes itself very seriously, and is dark in the extreme. Quite likely, Anthony Hinds' story (rewritten by screenwriter Batt) was becoming influenced by a horde of psycho-killer films coming from America at the time. Still bathed in the atmospheric settings of Victoriana, the film finds our Dr. Frankenstein more than obsessed, more than driven: now he's

Peter Cushing totes Susan Denberg, the "monster" of **FRANKENSTEIN CREATED WOMAN**

As Dr. Hertz in **FRANKENSTEIN CREATED WOMAN**, he was able to creatively weigh the character against Cushing's Frankenstein, showing great sympathy for both Hans and Christina… himself becoming a surrogate co-father figure (along with Cushing).

Danish poster for **FRANKENSTEIN MUST BE DESTROYED** (art by Rolf Goetze)

like a powerhouse of evil looking to corrupt in any way possible those whom he can exploit to aid him in his work. Possibly containing one of Cushing's finest performances on film, this is not the movie to watch if you want to see the kindly gentleman of horror at work! Rather, this is one to see for his range as an actor, and to see what evil, sinister vibes he can imbue his character with. Unlike the first film in the series, there's little cleavage-thrusting sexiness on view in this movie, although Veronica Carlson's Anna is certainly eye-catching enough (she was put to even better use in Freddie Francis' **DRACULA HAS RISEN FROM THE GRAVE** [1968, UK; see p.29], Clive Donner's **VAMPIRA** [a.k.a. **OLD DRACULA**, 1974], and Francis' **THE GHOUL** [1975, all UK]).

THE HORROR OF FRANKENSTEIN
UK, 1970. D/Wr: Jimmy Sangster
S: Ralph Bates, Kate O'Mara, Veronica Carlson, Jon Finch, Dennis Price, David Prowse

In Hammer's effort to reboot the series with a younger leading man, and to acknowledge the more sexually liberating times, they here tried (in retrospect, a one-off) to reinvent the series, to little critical or commercial acclaim.

Victor Frankenstein (Bates) is a soulless, womanizing but handsome young man who has inherited the family estate and monies by murdering his own father in order to gain the title of Baron. Now with money in his pockets, he goes abroad to attend medical school, but is expelled when he causes the dean's daughter to become pregnant. Obsessed with reviving the dead, he returns home and builds a laboratory, and, aided by a buxom maid, Alys (O'Mara), when he's not squeezing her flesh, he's thinking about creating a new life-form from death; which he does in the form of a bald, muscular creature played by future "Darth Vader" Dave Prowse. Of course this new younger version of the Baron also has another more "respectable" main squeeze named Elizabeth (Carlson), whom he considers making his bride...but Alys has much bigger tits, and looks like she would swallow a load without provocation. And, oh yes, there's also the *monster*! A pale, mute big guy who without much makeup probably was the cream-dream for many gay monster movie fans of the early '70s. Of course, being big and tall, Prowse—who was seen the following year in Kubrick's **A CLOCKWORK ORANGE** (1971, UK/USA)—could also leer, sneer and generally be menacing until his unfortunate drop into the acid bath at the finale, leaving Victor Frankenstein to start work anew on another creation.

Freddie Jones totes Peter Cushing in **FRANKENSTEIN MUST BE DESTROYED**

You Axed For It! Dave Prowse as the creature in **THE HORROR OF FRANKENSTEIN**, with chopper at the ready

Essentially a rewrite of **THE CURSE OF FRANKENSTEIN** with more sex, nudity, blood, and lots and *lots* of black humor, this intended reboot of the series falls flat in just about every category save titillation. Certainly, it's a watchable exercise, but little more than that. A movie about a spoiled, randy dandy who likes to experiment with dead bodies might be fine if it starred unknowns and was made by a low-budget sexploitation company. But this is Hammer, after all, and one expects quality all around; but **HORROR** is simply just not a very good film.

Ralph Bates was a talented and charismatic stage actor, who received decent critical notices for his television roles in historical costume dramas, which is where Hammer's people most likely discovered him. Thought to be the new young blood ushering in a wave of fresh, young, talented, and attractive leading men for Hammer's '70s films, Bates failed to catch on with audiences in any big way. He appeared in small but important roles in Peter Sasdy's **TASTE THE BLOOD OF DRACULA** (1970, UK [see p.31]), and Jimmy Sangster's **LUST FOR A VAMPIRE** (1971, UK) before really impressing audiences and critics alike with Roy Ward Baker's **DR. JEKYLL AND SISTER HYDE** (1971, UK), starring opposite Martine Beswick as the male half of the title pair. Bates also appeared in such lesser thrillers as Sangster's **FEAR IN THE NIGHT** (1972), Don Chaffey's **PERSECUTION** (1975), and Sasdy's **I DON'T WANT TO BE BORN** (a.k.a. **THE DEVIL WITHIN HER**, 1975, all UK), before returning to episodic television. He died at age 51 in 1991.

While photographed in Technicolor, the film stock was strangely reprocessed into lurid and dark "Metrocolor" by independent American distributor American Continental Films, Inc. Sharing a release (on a double-bill) with Roy Baker's **SCARS OF DRACULA** (1970, UK [see p.32]), this was the first Hammer film not widely distributed in the US and elsewhere by either Warner Bros., Universal, or another major distributor. EMI handled the domestic UK release. Possibly thought to be too lurid and sexy for the usual first-run theaters, **THE HORROR OF FRANKENSTEIN** was advertised with ugly and shoddy promotional posters, and quickly thrown into fleapit dives and drive-ins stateside.

Kate O'Mara was a shapely and very talented actress who worked a lot on the British stage and also on television. The present title is one of the comparatively few films in which she appeared, and Roy Baker's **THE VAMPIRE LOVERS** (1970, UK/USA) is another. Kate's petite frame, feline features and pronounced bust sure made her essential viewing for eye candy roles in a batch of classic British television shows like *The Avengers* (1961-69), *The Saint* (1967-68), *The Persuaders* and *Jason King* (both 1971-72). She passed away in March 2014, and, six months before this, I interviewed her, Martin Stephens (from Wolf Rilla's **VILLAGE OF THE DAMNED** [1960, UK]) and Damien Thomas (Count Karnstein in Hammer/John Hough's **TWINS OF EVIL** [1971, UK]); said interview can be seen at *https://www.youtube.com/watch?v=IBZuaCY5E_k*

FRANKENSTEIN AND THE MONSTER FROM HELL
UK, 1973/74. D: Terence Fisher
Wr: John Elder (Anthony Nelson Keys)
S: Peter Cushing, Shane Briant, Madeline Smith, Patrick Troughton, David Prowse

Carl Victor, alias Baron Victor Frankenstein (Cushing, natch!), is now living in an asylum. He's incarcerated there, but since it's known that he was a physician, he treats the other inmates. Dr. Klaus (John Stratton), who runs the asylum, is a corrupt blowhard who steals the fortunes of those who have been assigned to his "care"; he is also a pervert not above dallying with the shapely female inmates, and is someone whom Frankenstein has great disdain. Now aged, Frankenstein uses the surgical labs of the madhouse to continue his own experiments with reviving the dead, with more or less unfortunate results, and he's obviously grown a little mad himself. When Dr. Helder, a follower of Frankenstein's, is incarcerated for the crime of bodysnatching, he joins Frankenstein and his mute assistant, Sara; or the "Angel", as she's been dubbed by Frankenstein and others (she is played by innocent-eyed nubile Madeline Smith, also seen in Roy Baker's **THE VAMPIRE LOVERS** [1970, UK/USA], co-starring Cushing and late Hammer scream queen Ingrid Pitt [1937-2010]). We learn that Frankenstein's hands had been badly damaged in the fire that was the central climax of the film before last (i.e., **FRANKENSTEIN MUST BE DESTROYED**), so intricate surgeries requiring any great dexterity are now beyond his abilities.

Dr. Helder believes that the body parts Frankenstein has been using for his newest creation had been taken from those who died of natural causes, but learns that sometimes their deaths are organized by the doctor himself; usually those for which there is no cure, so there's a semblance of humanity in his madness. Frankenstein's newest creation is a hybrid monster made from parts of a hirsute, brutish murderer and a sculptor. The monster is a work-in-progress resembling some sort of ape-like creature, the result of some patchwork body part-stitching done with the assistance of Sara, whom it is learned became mute after her degenerate father (the asylum director) had raped her. When some new eyes and a brain are inserted into the creature, it goes on a violent rampage, murdering several patients and the director of the asylum before being literally torn to pieces by the lunatic residents.

In a solemn moment which fully reveals the madness that has taken over Frankenstein, and his assistants as well, they begin cleaning up after the destruction of the laboratory, planning to build a better monster.

A fitting if rather grim and somber end to a unique film series, **FRANKENSTEIN AND THE MONSTER FROM HELL** eschews the leering, tongue-in-cheek black comedy that was so badly shoehorned into the script for the only tenuously connected **HORROR OF FRANKENSTEIN**, as well as dispensing with the dense, dour and mean-spirited atmosphere that engulfed much of **FRANKENSTEIN MUST BE DESTROYED**, for a much more benign and yet still sinister approach. Wearing a very stylish, cool blonde-streaked-with-grey-and-white wig, Peter Cushing shines in every frame he's in. Only sixty years of age when the film was made, he plays Frankenstein with equal amounts sparkle and fragility. The film was director Fisher's career swan song, and one can see that he wanted to tie up loose thematic ends and come a bit full-circle: now that Frankenstein is incarcerated in an asylum and continuing his experiments, who is there to answer to, the lunatics or himself...?

Madeline Smith, with Dave Prowse—here playing a much more monstrous creature—in
FRANKENSTEIN AND THE MONSTER FROM HELL

DRACULA ACCORDING TO HAMMER

by Troy Howarth

Since its publication in 1897, Bram Stoker's *Dracula* has captured the imaginations of millions of readers. Film adaptations can be traced as far back as the now-lost **DRACULA'S DEATH** *(Dracula halála, 1921)*, produced in Austria and starring Paul Askonas as the title character. The most noteworthy adaptation of the silent era would prove to be an "unofficial" one, however: F.W. Murnau's **NOSFERATU, A SYMPHONY OF HORROR** *(Nosferatu, eine Symphonie des Grauens, 1922)* would land in court when the widow of Bram Stoker accused the filmmakers of plagiarism. The film was nearly destroyed for this reason, but happily some prints survived, and it is now regarded as a major benchmark in the horror genre.

Tod Browning's **DRACULA** *(1931, USA)* was adapted more from the stage adaptation by Hamilton Deane, and solidified the image of the courtly vampire in the form of Bela Lugosi. It was a role Lugosi played on stage, and he campaigned hard for the film—so hard, in fact, that he effectively put himself over a barrel for Universal Pictures to screw him over again and again as his career went through various peaks and valleys. Lugosi only played the role twice onscreen—the second time being Charles T. Barton's **ABBOTT AND COSTELLO MEET FRANKENSTEIN** *(1948, USA)*—but he played other vampires and vampire-like characters in films ranging from the sublime (Browning's **MARK OF THE VAMPIRE** *[1935, USA]*) to the disgraceful (Edward D. Wood, Jr.'s **PLAN 9 FROM OUTER SPACE** *[1959, USA]*). The Lugosi archetype became the stuff of parody after a certain point, and, by the 1950s, audiences had grown tired of cobwebbed crypts and pallid noblemen with Eurotrash accents.

Things started to change radically, however, in light of the international success of **THE CURSE OF FRANKENSTEIN** *(1957 [see p.11])*, produced by England's Hammer Films and directed by Terence Fisher (1904-1980). The film updated the Frankenstein mythos with the additions of blood, cleavage and lurid color, and its success proved that audiences were ready

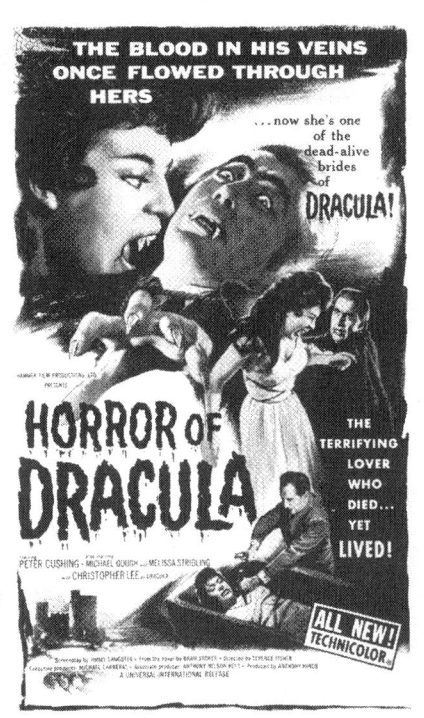

US pressbook ad for **DRACULA**, bearing the film's Stateside title

for more Gothic chills after the better part of a decade's worth of giant bugs and nuclear paranoia. Inevitably, in 1958 Hammer responded to the success by revisiting Dracula. It was a gamble that paid off in dividends: **DRACULA** (or, as it is known in the United States, **HORROR OF DRACULA**) would become another box-office sensation, and it also helped to make a star out of little-known character actor Christopher Lee.

Let's start off by stating the obvious: To say this film helped to define and shape the modern horror film is an understatement; it may not seem it now, but this was very strong stuff for its time, and it made a massive impression at box offices the world over. It also established Christopher Lee as the definitive Dracula for a new generation of viewers. As such, it is often referred to as Hammer's shining moment, as the indisputable jewel in the company's crown; in a sense, it has become a sacred cow—and like all sacred cows, it seems almost impossible to find any fault in it. Well, at the risk of sounding contrary—as if that has ever stopped me before!—I will go out on a limb and

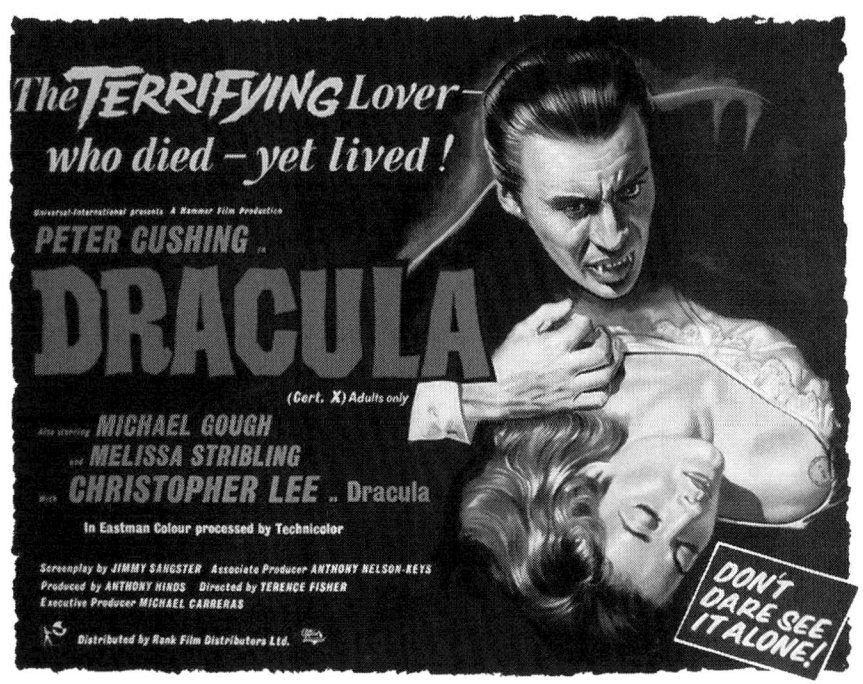

British poster

say that **DRACULA** is a damn good film—but it's not the flawless masterpiece some would make it out to be. There are some definite issues with Jimmy Sangster's screenplay; for example: in an attempt to avoid making the production too big and expansive, Sangster decided to have the action set in an ill-defined Mitteleuropa locale; fair enough, but the notion of the all-powerful, fearsome Count Dracula living a mere stone's throw away from the Holmwood residence, where so much of the second half of the picture takes place, does not make a lot of sense. Nobody outside of the village adjoining Castle Dracula seems to have ever heard of the man, and the superstitions surrounding vampire lore do not seem to have penetrated much beyond the village inn. There is also the peculiar notion of revising the character of Jonathan Harker (played here by John Van Eyssen, from **QUATERMASS 2** [1957, UK; see *Monster!* #11]) as a sort of understudy to Dr. Van Helsing (a pitch-perfect Peter Cushing, who requires no introduction): for some strange reason, Dracula has decided that he wants his library to be inventoried, and he falls for the bait and switch of having Harker come into his home to accomplish this goal. Unbeknownst to the Count, however, Harker is working with Van Helsing in order to eradicate the vampire and his minions. Why would Van Helsing entrust this task to a mere assistant? It makes precious little sense, nor does it bear close scrutiny that, knowing that he is working with very limited time, Harker would miss his opportunity to destroy the Count in favor of laying to rest the sexy vampire woman (Valerie Gaunt, from aforementioned **THE CURSE OF FRANKENSTEIN**) who has already infected him with the disease of vampirism. There's also a tremendous rush to keep the pace moving at such a fast clip, it sometimes gets in the way of establishing and maintaining a real sense of Gothic mood and atmosphere. On top of that, there's the intrusion of some very awkward comedy relief in the final reel—by contrast, the visit to quirky undertaker Miles Malleson (1888-1969; from Fisher's **THE HOUND OF THE BASKERVILLES** [1959, UK]) is a delight—which really strikes a particularly bad note during an otherwise-remarkable final act. Having dispensed with where the film goes wrong, however, it is equally important to discuss what the filmmakers got right—and happily, there's plenty of that on display.

Christopher Lee has very little screen time as the Count, thus establishing a precedent that will be followed through in the sequels, but he makes the most of every scene he is in. His Dracula is feral and frightening—he has often spoken of his desire to convey the pathos of the character, but I don't think he succeeds in that; he definitely is capable of conveying pathos without dialogue in films like both Fisher's own **THE CURSE OF FRANKEN-**

STEIN (1957, UK) and **THE MUMMY** (1959, UK), so it's not like he's not up to the task: instead, I think the truth of the matter is, he really latched onto the character's violent and imperious nature, and in that respect he made the character truly his own. Others have played the role brilliantly—Lugosi, Max Schreck, Klaus Kinski, Louis Jourdan, etc.—but for me, Lee *is* Dracula. Peter Cushing is his equal as the determined Dr. Van Helsing. The script is fairly one-dimensional with regards to his character, but Cushing makes it work: he is a single-minded obsessive, a sort of Captain Ahab on a quest to rid the world of evil, and he never strikes a false note. Unfortunately, the normally-reliable Michael Gough (Arthur Crabtree's **HORRORS OF THE BLACK MUSEUM** [1959, UK]) delivers quite a few false notes with his wooden portrayal of Arthur Holmwood, but Melissa Stribling (Basil Dearden's **THE LEAGUE OF GENTLEMEN** [1960, UK]), Carol Marsh (Brian Desmond Hurst's **A CHRISTMAS CAROL** [1951, UK]) and the aforementioned Gaunt all make a vivid impression as the women who fall under Dracula's spell.

With its luminous color photography by Jack Asher and its impressive sets by Bernard Robinson, **DRACULA** looks a lot more expensive than it really was. Director Terence Fisher creates some poetic flourishes—notably the use of swirling leaves to announce the Count's arrival, a touch he would recycle in later films, including **THE GORGON** (1964, UK)—and tells the story with authority. Fisher, a journeyman who toiled on many undistinguished potboilers for the first decade of his directing career, came into his own with these Hammer-produced Gothics; he displayed a flair for the genre and took the work very seriously, something which could not be said of many of the directors employed by Hammer. James Bernard's score is arguably a little *too* blood-and-thunder—I prefer his work on some of the sequels, frankly—but it seems to be the score the film requires. It all builds to a climax that is truly among the most powerful and effective in the history of the genre.

Following the success of **DRACULA**, Hammer took a while to devise a sequel. Rumors abound about the reasons for this, but the stars finally aligned when the company produced Fisher's **DRACULA – PRINCE OF DARKNESS** (1966, UK). Prior to this, they had made the same director's **THE BRIDES OF DRACULA** (1960, UK), a Dracula-less entry which continued the adventures of Peter Cushing's Van Helsing; it was arguably the best film of the lot, but, given that Dracula isn't in it (its vampire is a rather fey one by the name of Baron Meinster, played with relish by David Peel [1920-1981] in the role of his short-lived film career), it falls outside the scope of this discussion.

In **DRACULA – PRINCE OF DARKNESS**, a group of travelers is stranded at Castle Dracula; the Count's mysterious servant offers them hospitality, and they are put up for the night. One of the group is slaughtered and his blood is used to revive the Count, who proceeds to go on a blood-drinking rampage...

This, the first sequel, remains Hammer horror at its finest—and it is undoubtedly the best of their Dracula films to actually feature the Count. Unlike the breathless 1958 original, this one takes its time to build mood and atmosphere. The film is nearly halfway finished when Dracula (Christopher Lee, of course) finally makes his entrance. But don't let that put you off: the time is well-spent, establishing characters worth caring about and building up mood and suspense in a most expert manner. Terence Fisher is at his very best in these early scenes, as he takes the time to tease things out, prowling the castle with his camera and creating a sense of an evil presence waiting to return. The resurrection scene is justifiably famous: Hammer wasn't exactly noted for their state-of-the-art special effects, but Les Bowie (1913-1979) outdid himself here. Once Dracula is back, things settle into a more routine pattern, but Lee is simply magnificent as he lunges into attack mode; his Dracula is even more feral and animalistic this

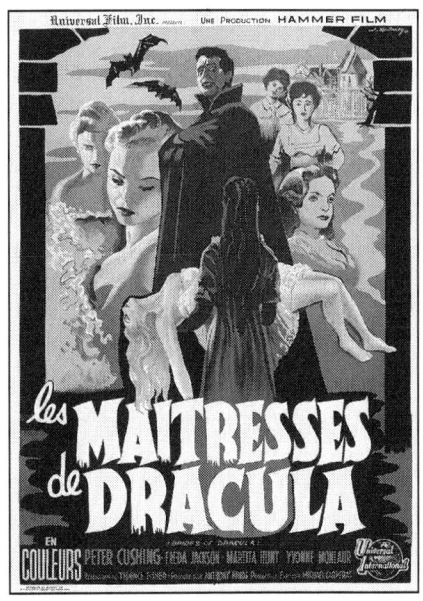

French poster for **THE BRIDES OF DRACULA** (art by J. Koutachy)

Italian *locandina* for **DRACULA - PRINCE OF DARKNESS** (art by Enzo Nistri)

time around. The actor would later claim that he refused to say the dialogue provided as it was too terrible, but I am inclined to believe screenwriter Jimmy Sangster (1927-2011): there was never any dialogue written for the character. If you look at the film, this makes sense: Dracula returns, hungry for blood, and doesn't really have an opportunity to speak when he is onscreen. Sooner than view the absence of dialogue as a negative, I view it as a plus: it makes the character even more frightening and phantom-like, making this arguably Lee's most effective crack at the character for Hammer.

In addition to Lee, the film is graced with a top-notch ensemble. **DRACULA** may have suffered from a truly wooden turn by Michael Gough, but this particular ensemble is beyond reproach. Barbara Shelley (**THE GORGON**) is brilliant as the repressed Englishwoman who falls victim to Dracula and turns into a sexually wanton vampire. Andrew Keir (1926-1997; **QUATERMASS AND THE PIT**, a.k.a. **FIVE MILLION YEARS TO EARTH** [1967, UK; see *Monster!* #11]) is fantas- tic as the no-nonsense Father Sandor—any concerns over the absence of Peter Cushing are laid to rest early on when Keir arrives on scene and takes command of the screen. Sandor is a very interesting character and I wish he could have had a series of screen adventures of his own; for my money, he is an even more engaging character than Van Helsing. The normally bland "young couple" characters are played by Francis Matthews (1927-2014; **THE REVENGE OF FRANKENSTEIN** [1958, UK]; see p.15) and Suzan Farmer (**RASPUTIN: THE MAD MONK** [1965, UK]), and they are charming and likable. Charles Tingwell (1923-2009; **'BREAKER' MORANT**, 1980, Australia) and Thorley Walters (1913-1991; **THE PHANTOM OF THE OPERA** [1962, UK]) lend solid support, and there's a marvelous performance from Philip Latham (**THE DEVIL-SHIP PIRATES** [1964, UK]) as Klove, Dracula's slightly musty servant. Dracula had been free of a human minion in the original film, but screenwriter Jimmy Sangster (hiding behind the *nom de plume* of John Sansom, as he was not thrilled with the end result) decided to go back to Stoker and introduce not one, but two variants on the Renfield character: Klove is the Count's right-hand man, removing obstacles and helping to protect him during the daylight hours, while the imprisoned Ludwig (played by Walters) also helps to advance his cause and has a taste for eating insects, to boot.

By this stage, Jack Asher (1916-1991) had left Hammer due to his time-consuming methods, but Michael Reed (born 1929) proved to be an inspired replacement for a far-too-brief period; he would soon be supplanted by the efficient but less-inspired Arthur Grant (1915-1972). Reed's lighting is absolutely gorgeous, making this arguably the best-looking film in the series. The sets by Bernard Robinson (1912-1970) are again effective at making the film look bigger than it really was, while Fisher and Reed make excellent use of the widescreen process to give it that sense of scope. The music by James Bernard (1925-2001) reprises many elements from his score for **DRACULA**, but I find it an altogether subtler and more pleasing soundtrack; I wish it were available on CD.

Of course, those viewers who preferred the fast-and-furious thrills of **DRACULA** tend to find **DRACULA – PRINCE OF DARKNESS** to be a bit of a slog. There is also the inevitable criticism that it's lacking Peter Cushing, and the oft-repeated urban legend about Christopher Lee being so dissatisfied with the dialogue that he refused to speak it. As already mentioned, there is something to be said for the slow pacing of this film: it allows one to savor the atmosphere, and it also gives the actors a better opportunity to establish their characters. Van Helsing may be gone, but there is nothing shabby about Father Sandor as a replacement: with his earthy humor and bull-in-a-china shop attitude, he makes for an imposing foe for the king of the vampires. As for the lack of dialogue on Dracula's part, it's hard to ascertain just when Christopher Lee started making these claims; like so many great actors and raconteurs, Lee is not above "embroidering" on the truth every now and again. Sangster always claimed that he didn't say anything in the film because the character never had any dialogue—and I, for one, believe him. It could well be that Lee was confusing the film with some of the sequels, where he did strike a number of lines from the scripts. In this particular adventure, however, let's be honest: there really isn't anywhere for the Count to do any yakking! The character is all the more effective for it: as presented in this film, Lee's Dracula is at his most feral and frightening.

DRACULA – PRINCE OF DARKNESS was another big money-maker for Hammer, so they wasted comparatively little time in getting Lee back to play his most popular character. **DRACULA HAS RISEN FROM THE GRAVE** emerged in 1968, and it would prove to be the most successful film of the series, commercially-speaking. The American distributors, Warner Brothers, devised a campy ad campaign, which probably helped. I have probably seen this film more times than any other movie. As a kid, I was absolutely obsessed with it. I can still probably recite much of the dialogue to this day. Oddly, for a film I know and enjoy so much, I wouldn't make any grand claims for it: the screenplay by Anthony Hinds has some illogicalities, and it can be argued that it marks the place where Hammer went from making films for adults to making films for a more teen-based demographic. There are also some really sloppy continuity errors. Even so, I find it to be arguably the most purely entertaining entry in the series.

In a nutshell, the action kicks off when a cowardly priest (Ewan Hooper) enlists the aid of the monsignor (Rupert Davies) to perform an exorcism on Castle Dracula. The ceremony goes off without a hitch, but the priest flees in terror and inadvertently aids in resurrecting Dracula when he falls on top of the Count's icy grave: blood flowing from a wound on his forehead seeps into a crack in the ice and the Count is up and running once more. Furious that his castle has been "defiled", Dracula forces the priest to lead him to the monsignor's village, where he plans to wreak havoc by targeting the old man's lovely niece, Maria (Veronica Carlson)...

Terence Fisher was originally slated to direct,

Down For The Count: Chris Lee, looking less than his best, in **DRACULA HAS RISEN FROM THE GRAVE**

but a game of drunken chicken with oncoming traffic put that plan to rest; in his place, cinematographer-turned-director Freddie Francis (1917-2007) brings a much less weighty approach to the material. Fisher's background was in editing, so his films tended to be more reliant on montage, while Francis' more visual background prompted him to experiment with more audacious and gimmicky angles. Francis' approach is rather pop art compared to Fisher's classicism, but it works well enough in context. He also inspires the normally rather reserved cinematographer Arthur Grant to cut loose and be a little more experimental than

Lookin' For A Kiss: The Count cozies up to Veronica Carlson in **GRAVE**

usual with color. Grant's decision to reuse Francis' amber filters from Jack Clayton's **THE INNOCENTS** (1961, USA/UK)—on which Francis provided some extraordinary black-and-white cinematography—has inspired equal measures of praise and criticism: some find it a clumsy device, while others find it quite beautiful. I'm somewhere in between: it works well in some shots, but looks a bit cheesy in others. In any event, the film looks terrific: Bernard Robinson did his last sets for a Dracula film on this picture, and they are up to his usual standards, and Francis and Grant provide some beautiful imagery along the way.

This was the beginning of Christopher Lee's disenchantment with the franchise, and one can understand why: the character of Dracula is sidelined for much of the action and is largely confined to a musty cellar, thus setting a trend followed in later entries. As in the first two entries, however, he makes the best of the material provided to him, and I love his look in this film: makeup artists Heather Nurse (who would go on to work on **SCARS OF DRACULA** [1970, UK; see below]) and Rosemary McDonald-Peattie (whose only other credit seems to be the Peter Cushing cheapie **THE BLOOD BEAST TERROR** [a.k.a. **THE VAMPIRE-BEAST CRAVES BLOOD**, 1967, UK]) provide probably the best bloodshot contact lenses of the franchise, and the silvery wig is very good, too—if only more care had been taken with the glue, which tends to crease rather obviously in the more intense close-ups. Much of Lee's dialogue is monosyllabic drivel—"There is a girl. Bring her to me."—but it's better than what he would be saddled with in the next entry. Crucially, he here plays the role with some energy and enthusiasm, and is properly scary; his next two cracks at the role (for Hammer, in any case) look a bit sluggish and ill-humored by comparison.

The supporting cast is headed by Rupert Davies, who plays the monsignor who serves as the Van Helsing figure. Davies was playing quite a few clerical types in horror movies during this time: he can also be seen as a man of the cloth in both Vernon Sewell's **CURSE OF THE CRIMSON ALTAR** (a.k.a. **THE CRIMSON CULT**) and Michael Reeves' **WITCHFINDER GENERAL** (a.k.a. **THE CONQUEROR WORM**, both 1968, UK). The character starts off as rather stuffy and intolerant, but Davies provides him with warmth and some sly humor. The beautiful Veronica Carlson (**FRANKENSTEIN MUST BE DESTROYED** [1969, UK; see p.18]) is very good as his niece, who becomes the object of Dracula's vengeance, while Barry Andrews (**THE BLOOD**

Above: Valerie van Ost as one of the Count's top-popping vampire brides gets staked by Michael Coles in **THE SATANIC RITES OF DRACULA**. **Top:** Voracious, voluptuous vampiress Anoushka Hempel about to chomp on Christopher Matthews' jugular in **SCARS OF DRACULA**.

ON SATAN'S CLAW [1970, UK]) does a solid job as her atheist boyfriend. Francis spends a good deal of time with these characters, and the end result is a film of uncommon warmth: it may do the central character a disservice in a way, but they feel like real people and their interactions seem genuine. This is definitely key to the film's appeal. Barbara Ewing is very impressive as the seductive barmaid who vies for Andrews' attentions, and Michael Ripper has one of his better roles as a cheery innkeeper/bartender.

It may not reinvent the wheel—I've always felt that it goes downhill a bit after Davies is sidelined, and the plot device of making "non-believer" Paul "see the light" is as ridiculous as it is insulting, though the finale is certainly robust enough—but **DRACULA HAS RISEN FROM THE GRAVE** is wonderful "comfort" viewing. I still enjoy it immensely.

With Christopher Lee becoming more and more disenchanted with Hammer's *Dracula* sequels, plans were in the works to make a Dracula film with another actor. Hammer cast their eyes towards a younger man named Ralph Bates, but when Warner Bros. got word that they were planning to do a Dracula film without their number one star, they made it clear: no Christopher Lee, no distribution from Warner Bros. Hammer's head honcho Sir James Carreras (1910-1990) then sweet-talked Lee into coming back, and he did so with grave reservations, not the least because the title struck him as tacky in the extreme. Fair enough on that end, but in all other respects **TASTE THE BLOOD OF DRACULA** (1970, UK) is a Grade "A" Hammer Horror.

The story by Anthony Hinds (1922-2013) has some muddled points—how was Dracula supposed to come back if not by inhabiting his minion's body? Thus, why does he feel the need to get revenge on the men who killed said minion?—but if we overlook these leaps in logic it offers up a rich and interesting scenario. A trio of supposedly respectable but actually morally degenerate gentlemen—beautifully played by Geoffrey Keen (**THE SPY WHO LOVED ME** [1977, UK]), John Carson (**THE PLAGUE OF THE ZOMBIES** [1966, UK; see *Monster!* #10]) and Peter Sallis (Wallace & Gromit's *The Wrong Trousers* [1993, UK])—decide to indulge in a black mass for some kicks. Lord Courtley (Bates, demoted to lackey status) heads up the ritual, which utilizes the powdered blood and relics belonging to Count Dracula. The gentlemen chicken-out and kill Courtley, leaving Dracula to regenerate himself in Courtley's body. The Count then proceeds to get revenge through the children of the three men.

Lee has very little to do here and signs of boredom are visible in his performance, but he still strikes an imposing figure. If only Hinds and director Peter Sasdy hadn't elected to end each of the three killings with a tight close-up of Dracula grimly intoning, "The First", "The Second", and "The Third". Yeah, we get it, Count Von Count! It gets very silly by the second time, and provokes laughs on the third…but this is a rare misstep in an otherwise beautifully crafted movie. Lee's appearance is a little more "youthful" compared to the previous entries, but this could perhaps be explained by his inhabiting the body of his younger minion.

The supporting cast is terrific: Carson, Keen and Sallis are marvelous actors in general, and they really bring a lot of class to the production. Carson becomes the *de facto* vampire savant figure, and he is the only one of the three men who is viewed in a more sympathetic manner—after all, he is a widower and he's not really out cheating on his spouse when the three of them go off for their monthly visit to the local whorehouse. Sallis is the coward of the group, and plays that angle beautifully, while Keen—often squandered in dull authority roles—is marvelously perverse as the bully of the trio. The young leads are very well played by Linda Hayden and Anthony Corlan/Higgins. They make for a likable pair of star-crossed lovers, and they have a weight to them that is lacking

Lee's Drac was cover boy of this 1974 British book by Alan Frank, which is fondly remembered by many a baby boomer Monster Kid

in some of the other youthful lover figures in other Hammer horrors of the period. Gwen Watford, Roy Kinnear, Russell Hunter and Michael Ripper are all excellent in their respective roles, while Hammer's would-be "replacement Lee", Ralph Bates, has his best role for the company—he plays it very over-the-top, but it suits the character very well. It's a pity Hammer would cast him in rather uninteresting roles for much of his time with them, as this one—and the later **DR. JEKYLL AND SISTER HYDE** (1971, UK)—demonstrates that he had a flair for this sort of thing and could do well with the right material and the right director to prod him along.

Peter Sasdy (born 1935), a Hungarian émigré making his feature directing debut, handles the material with a sensitivity not to be found in the series outside of the ones directed by Terence Fisher. He has a good sense of pace and knows how to build atmosphere. Sasdy would fulfill the promise shown here with two more Hammer productions—the uneven **COUNTESS DRACULA** (1971, UK) and the superb **HANDS OF THE RIPPER** (1971, UK)—as well as the superior British TV ghost story **THE STONE TAPE** (1972), but his later work—including the inept **I DON'T WANT TO BE BORN** (a.k.a. **THE DEVIL WITHIN HER**, 1976, UK) and **THE LONELY LADY** (1983, USA)—proved to be disappointing. The production has ample gloss, thanks to Arthur Grant's cinematography and the Scott MacGregor (1914-1971) production design. And James Bernard's score is truly one of his best.

TASTE THE BLOOD OF DRACULA has its flaws, but it remains one of Hammer's best vampire films. The excellent performances, classy production values and intriguing storyline make it a stand-out in the series.

Hammer wasted no time in going back to the drawing-board, and **SCARS OF DRACULA** (1970, UK) displays all the signs of having been assembled with indecent haste. Many lazy journalists and hipster filmgoers insist upon calling Hammer's product "campy", but this is generally a major misnomer; here, however, the term has some merit.

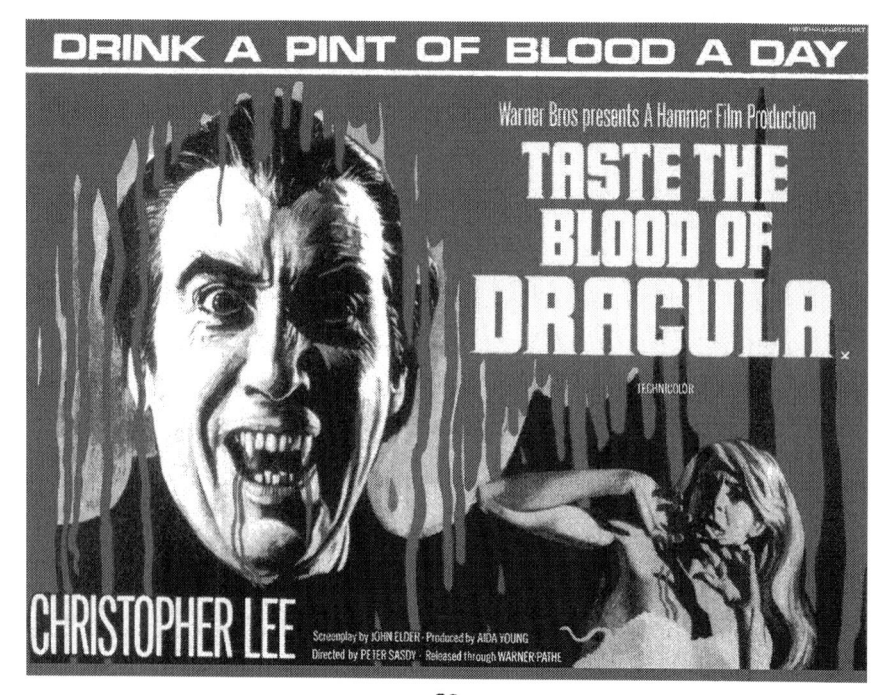

This is the sleazy, seedy, grindhouse Dracula film of the Hammer series. In an effort to reboot the franchise, Anthony Hinds disregards continuity and has the Count resurrected in his castle. Things kick off on an…*interesting*…note, as a fake-looking rubber bat vomits blood over the Count's ashes, prompting some footage of his disintegration in **TASTE THE BLOOD OF DRACULA** to be run in reverse, thus allowing Christopher Lee to return to life. From there, there's some good stuff as a village girl is found dead in the fields and the villagers storm the castle…but then we get bogged-down in some bedroom farce material as we are introduced to our insufferable young leads. The rest is a very mixed bag, featuring a little more screen time for Lee than usual and some arresting moments of unbridled sadism.

I don't mind that the film is more violent and exploitative than its predecessors. On that level, the film is successful enough in its aims: it's the one film in the series that goes for the gore, and it delivers on that score. What I do mind is the utterly dismal look of the film coupled with the flat and listless direction by Roy Ward Baker (1916-2010). Baker was a very good journeyman whose career highlights included the best film about the Titanic (**A NIGHT TO REMEMBER** [1958, UK]), and one of Hammer's finest films—the above-cited **QUATERMASS AND THE PIT**. He never seemed all that well-suited to Gothic horror, however, and his handling of this material is especially uninspired. He works in the odd flourish, but for the most part his coverage is very basic and lacking in atmosphere. The lighting by Moray Grant (1917-1977) is, in a word, ugly. The makeup effects on the various unlucky villagers savaged to death by Dracula and his minion, the rubber bat, are pretty good—but poor Lee looks like a pantomime Dracula this time around. Coupled with Lee's obvious boredom this time out, the end result only serves to make the character look like a shadow of his former self. He does however spring to life during the various violent scenes—I will give him that. Then there are the sets to contend with: bearing in mind that the castle is supposed to be in bad shape following a fire, it still looks remarkably cheap and spare. This extends to the other sets as well. I gather that the budget was not appreciably cheaper than in the previous entries, so I can only blame this on the lighting; perhaps a little more care with the shadows would have made the sets look a little better or the background matte paintings a little less obvious.

In addition to Lee's admittedly unenthusiastic performance, the film is also burdened with the least interesting "young leads" in any Hammer horror film. Dennis Waterman (*The Sweeney* [1975-78, UK]) and Christopher Matthews (Gordon Hessler's **SCREAM AND SCREAM AGAIN** [1970, UK]) are competent actors, but they seem badly cast; Baker later said that they should have swapped roles, and I suspect he was right. Jenny Hanley (Pete Walker's **THE FLESH AND BLOOD SHOW** [1972, UK]) is pretty, but her performance is compromised by being dubbed by another actress; why the decision was made to do this is anybody's business, but then, Hammer was in the bad habit of looping actors, often without their knowledge. The trio of Patrick Troughton

Big Drac Attack: The Count does the nasty to Patrick Troughton—scorching the skin off his back with a bloomin' saber!—in **SCARS OF DRACULA**, the nastiest, cheapest and trashiest of Hammer's *Dracula* saga

(Richard Donner's **THE OMEN** [1976, USA/UK]), Michael Gwynn (Wolf Rilla's **VILLAGE OF THE DAMNED** [1960, UK]) and Michael Ripper (John Gilling's **THE MUMMY'S SHROUD** [1966, UK]) give the best performances, by far. Gwynn is effective as the ineffectual priest who seems poised to become a Van Helsing figure, but ultimately does little to advance the action; there's an interesting revisionist idea here in questioning elder authority figures, but not much is made of it. Ripper has far and away the *surliest* role of his career, but he plays it very well. Troughton (1920-1987), a splendid character actor—best-known for playing *Doctor Who* from 1966-69—labors behind a tacky makeup job with troglodyte eyebrows and a shaggy wig (and speaking of wigs, the one on Gwynn is positively comical; the poor man looks like he will crumble under the weight of it!), and sometimes resorts to hammy mannerisms, but he is otherwise very effective as Dracula's dimwitted retainer, Klove. Unlike the smooth and elegant Philip Latham in the above **DRACULA – PRINCE OF DARKNESS**, Troughton is closer to the old-school monster minion one would expect in a '40s Universal outing. Troughton participates in the film's kinkiest scene, in which the Count brands him with a red-hot sword for disobeying his orders, thus providing the film with its title; Troughton reportedly kept a still of this scene in hanging on his bathroom wall!

SCARS OF DRACULA is best appreciated as a piece of trashy pulp, but for all its enthusiasm in going for the grimy and exploitative, I just wish it could have been directed with a bit more flair or rendered with a little more production polish. As it stands, it comes off as not only the nastiest of the series—but the most amateurish, as well.

Following **SCARS OF DRACULA**—which failed to secure distribution from Warner Bros., who were reportedly dismayed by the film's cheapjack production values—Hammer decided to copy the Americans by putting vampires in the modern era. Inspired by the success of Bob Kelljan's scary no-budgeter **COUNT YORGA, VAMPIRE** (1970, USA), starring Robert Quarry in the title role, they concocted a scenario whereby Christopher Lee's Dracula could be brought into the modern day. Lee was not necessarily thrilled with the idea, but when various projects he committed to in 1971 went down the tubes he elected to take the money and run. The result was **DRACULA A.D. 1972** (1972, UK), probably Hammer's most controversial Dracula film.

A pre-credits sequence allows for some appropriately Gothic imagery as Dracula and Van Helsing (Peter Cushing, finally returning to the Hammer Dracula fold after many years' absence) battle to the death on a runaway carriage. It's a gripping opening, very well-directed by Alan Gibson (1938-1987). From there, Gibson pulls a Kubrick by panning from the 19th Century to the 20th, as a plane flies overheard announcing that we are no longer in Hammer's usual milieu. A hopelessly protracted party sequence featuring The Stoneground (sue me, but I enjoy their songs just fine!) slows things down a bit, but it eventually regains its footing as Dracula's minion Johnny Alucard (Christopher Neame, from Jimmy Sangster's **LUST FOR A VAMPIRE** [1970, UK]) convinces a group of spaced-out kids—including Van Helsing's own granddaughter, Jessica (Stephanie Beacham, from Michael Winner's **THE NIGHTCOMERS** [1971, UK], co-starring Brando)—to participate in a black mass. Despite the fact that these kids are the oldest group of "teenage" delinquents this side of *Beverly Hills 90210*, Gibson and cinematographer Dick Bush (1931-1997) make a great set-piece out of the black mass as Neame's overacting goes positively into hyper-drive and gorgeous Caroline Munro volunteers to become Dracula's first victim. With Lee back in the picture and Cushing back on the case trying to bring him down, it settles into classic good-versus-evil, Hammer-style, and it's done with such energy and style I find myself forgiving its missteps. In terms of sheer entertainment value, **DRACULA A.D. 1972** is up there with my most rewatched entries in the series. It also helps that Cushing gives what I deem to be his best performance as Van Helsing here—compared to the rather one-dimensional zealot conceived by Jimmy Sangster in the 1958 original, this Van Helsing wrestles with some inner doubts and he is also motivated by something a little more humane than just a desire to eradicate evil: he is also looking to protect the granddaughter on whom

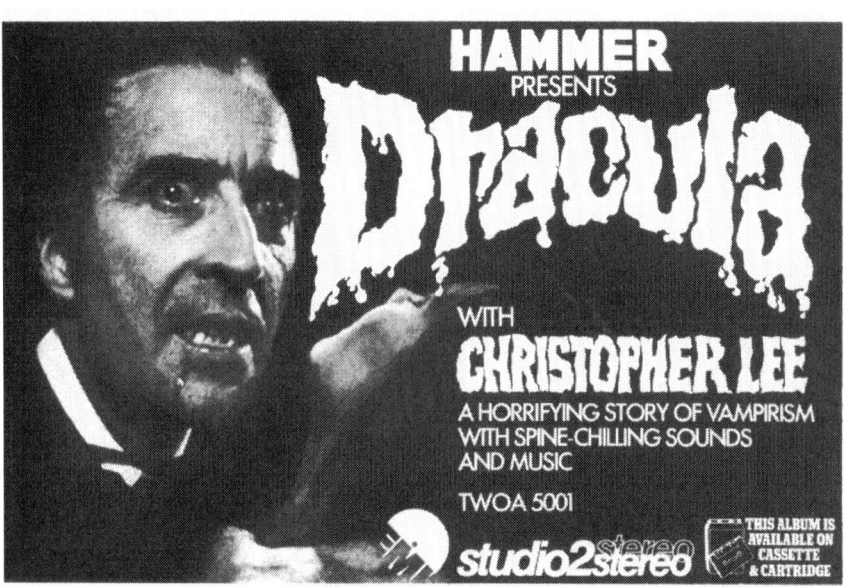

This trade ad for an early-'70s spoken-word audio dramatization ran in such British genre periodicals as *The House of Hammer* and *World of Horror*. The still used is from **DRACULA A.D. 1972**, and the vampire's victim is Caroline Munro

he dotes. The story goes that Cushing was originally intended to be Jessica's father, but that he aged so drastically following the death of his wife Helen in early 1971 that the filmmakers worried he looked too old to fill that role—so he became a grandfather instead. Cushing, always a thin man, looks gaunt and vaguely haunted, but his energy is undiminished. His good friend Christopher Lee, who looked vaguely bored and disenchanted in the last two entries, seems to have felt energized by Cushing's return: he rises to the occasion, and is arguably at his *scariest* in this picture. Their two big showdowns are terrific to behold, and should be enough to warm the heart of any Hammer film aficionado. It may not be Great Art, but it is Fun Entertainment indeed!

DRACULA A.D. 1972 didn't set the box office on fire, but Hammer launched into a sequel before they realized the writing was on the wall: audiences were simply no longer interested in repackaged goods and were looking for fresh, new horror films like Roman Polanski's **ROSEMARY'S BABY** and George A. Romero's **NIGHT OF THE LIVING DEAD** (both 1968, USA), and William Friedkin's **THE EXORCIST** (1973, USA). With **THE SATANIC RITES OF DRACULA** (a.k.a. **COUNT DRACULA AND HIS VAMPIRE BRIDE**, 1973, UK), screenwriter Don Houghton (1930-1991) devised a much more ingenious scenario and Hammer brought Alan Gibson back to put Cushing and Lee through their paces—the latter for the very last time in a Hammer Dracula film.

This time out, an occult society headed by the mysterious D.D. Denham—come on, is there ever any doubt who *he* really is?!—is wielding great political power in modern England. When a series of bizarre murders attracts the attention of the police and the British secret service, Van Helsing (Cushing, naturally) is drafted in to help investigate. Van Helsing's worst fears are confirmed when he realizes that Dracula has risen from the grave once more—and it's time for one final showdown as Jessica (Joanna Lumley, later of the long-running Britcom *Absolutely Fabulous* [1992-2012]) is again caught in the crossfire.

In a sense, **THE SATANIC RITES OF DRACULA** plays like a horror-themed episode of the classic British TV series *The Avengers* (1961-69)—hardly a stretch, since Cushing and Lee both did guest stints, and Lumley would go on to play one of the leads in the short-lived *The New Avengers* (1976-77, UK/France/Canada). Dracula is more like a shadowy James Bond villain this time out—fittingly enough, Lee would go on to star as Scaramanga, **THE MAN WITH THE GOLDEN GUN** (1974, UK), not long after this—while Van Helsing is somewhat sidelined in favor of Inspector Murray (Michael Coles, reprising his role from **DRACULA A.D. 1972**) and

"Postdated" Belgian poster for **DRACULA A.D. 1972** (art unsigned)

Torrance from MI5 (William Franklyn, from Polanski's **CUL-DE-SAC** [1966, UK]). There are some great scenes to be had here, however, as Van Helsing confronts a disgraced colleague (a marvelously jittery Freddie Jones, from David Lynch's **THE ELEPHANT MAN** [1980, USA/UK]), who has been roped into developing a new strain of the bubonic plague for the vengeance-and-suicide-minded Dracula; as well as the final showdown between Dracula and Van Helsing. It's a clever story, well-executed by Gibson and his talented team of technicians, and it benefits from a very good cast: Lee and Cushing are professional as ever, while Jones, Franklyn, Coles and Lumley all lend excellent support.

With this entry, Christopher Lee finally bid adieu to the role that made him a star. Some have criticized his disdain for the sequels, suggesting that he was biting the hand that fed him, but he has never objected to the role or the source material—merely to the way that Hammer's screenwriters marginalized him as the sequels wore on. Even Peter Cushing understood where he was coming from, rightly noting that the part seldom gave Lee a chance to do anything but glower and spout monosyllabic dialogue. He made the part his own, however, and even at his least inspired, he *IS* Dracula for me. The subsequent years would find him going through various peaks and valleys in his career, but he is still with us and has been appearing in major motion pictures into his '90s; a back injury sustained on the set of his Hammer "return", **THE RESIDENT** (2010, UK/USA), has slowed him down, and I don't think we can look forward to seeing him physically appearing in any more pictures—but his still-magnificent voice remains strong and he continues to do some vocal work...as well as some controversial singing, which is not really my cup of tea, but what the hell: long may he continue! As for Cushing, he would return to the series one last time, this time facing-off against a new (and inferior) performer in the role of the Prince of Darkness...

After the experiment of updating Dracula to the modern era failed to strike box office gold, the desperate producers at Hammer decided to try another course of action: kung fu films had become big business, so why not combine vampires with martial arts? A deal was reached with Sir Run Run Shaw (1907-2014), and Hammer sent veteran director Roy Ward Baker off to Hong Kong to direct—along with his co-director, Shaws' kung fu master Chang Cheh—what would become the last of the Hammer *Dracula* films to date: **THE LEGEND OF THE 7 GOLDEN VAMPIRES** (七金屍 / *Qi jin shi*, 1974, UK/HK). Truth be told, it did not start off as a Dracula film, however; in an attempt to woo Warner Bros. (who did decide to release the film in the UK, though a US release would not be forthcoming through them), a decision was reached to shoehorn Dracula into the plot. This had long been Christopher Lee's complaint with the sequels—that the character had been added in as an afterthought—and there was no way he was going to go back on his decision to leave the franchise. In his place, character actor John Forbes-Robertson (Piers Haggard's and Tobe Hooper's **VENOM** [1981, UK]) was brought in to appear in some bookend scenes as the Lord of the Undead. Sadly, the makeup artists overdid things rather badly, and he looks more like the drag queen of the undead...and, in a final indignity, Forbes-Robertson was incensed to find out that his entire performance was redubbed by David De Keyser. In that sense, it's hard to really assess his performance fairly...but he doesn't make the same impression as Lee, no matter how you look at it, though he is given a good deal more dialogue than Lee had been in some of his entries. Oh well, no matter—Dracula is barely a presence here, anyway.

The story deals with a vampire cult which is terrorizing a small village in China. Professor Van Helsing (Cushing, of course) though having been killed off in 1872, per **DRACULA A.D. 1972**, he is still in fine fighting fettle!—is called in to assist a family in combating the creatures. Ultimately, Van Helsing realizes that his old foe, Count Dracula (Forbes-Robertson) is connected to it all...

Baker handles the material with considerably more flair and style than he had on **SCARS OF DRACULA**. The movie rattles along at a good pace, and the lighting by John Wilcox (1905-1979) and Roy Ford is awash with Mario Bava-esque reds and greens. The story may be ridiculous and some of the acting on the stilted side, but it delivers where it counts: the horror scenes have a nightmarish quality to them—the inclusion of Chinese "hopping" *jiangshi* ghouls in the Hammer universe

A very rare Shaw Brothers' magazine ad for **DRACULA AND THE 7 GOLDEN VAMPIRES** (sic)

is a novel touch—and the kung fu sequences are well-staged and -executed. Peter Cushing brings his usual class and professionalism to a role he could easily have walked through by this stage. He dominates the proceedings quite handily, though David Chiang (r.n. Wei-Nien Chiang) is also engaging as the young man who is determined to rid his village of the vampires. James Bernard—his name misspelled in the opening titles as Benard—contributes another rousing score, though this time there are liberal "borrowed" helpings from his earlier scores for **FRANKENSTEIN MUST BE DESTROYED, TASTE THE BLOOD OF DRACULA** and **SCARS OF DRACULA**, indicating that he probably had a little less time than usual to complete the assignment.

THE LEGEND OF THE 7 GOLDEN VAMPIRES did decent business in the UK, but for whatever reason Warner elected not to put the film out in the US. It would eventually be picked up by a smaller label, Dynamite Entertainment (headed by Milton Subotsky [1921-1991], the former co-head of Amicus, who had been Hammer's chief competitor in the 1960s and early '70s), who released it in a heavily reedited version titled **THE SEVEN BROTHERS MEET DRACULA**. It may not be the classiest note to end the series on, but no matter: it's an imaginative and entertaining little movie, and if it doesn't quite manage to successfully fuse Eastern and Western mythology, it scores bonus points for trying something new.

In the years since Hammer discontinued their *Dracula* franchise, others have tried their hand at the character. Werner Herzog made a magnificent remake of **NOSFERATU THE VAMPYRE** (*Nosferatu: Phantom der Nacht*, 1979, West Germany/France), with the great Klaus Kinski giving a remarkable performance as Dracula, while the BBC delivered a fantastic 2-part miniseries called *Count Dracula* (1977, UK), which featured Louis Jourdan as a smooth and sardonic Count. The big-budget Universal remake from 1979 with Frank Langella and Laurence Olivier gets knocked a lot, but it's a worthy film nonetheless. Francis Ford Coppola's attempt at a "faithful" adaptation—**BRAM STOKER'S DRACULA** (1992, USA)—was bedeviled by hubris, a corny love story and some badly miscast actors. Most of these later films were shot on budgets which were far more lavish than any Hammer ever had to work with—and yet, with the exception of the Herzog and BBC versions, most of them failed to come close to recapturing the special magic of the Hammer series. For this viewer, at least, there's simply no topping Christopher Lee and Peter Cushing in these iconic characterizations.

In **THE LEGEND OF THE 7 GOLDEN VAMPIRES**, on his Transylvanian home turf, the rather foppish and over-made-up "new" Count Dracula (John Forbes-Robertson) is about to infect the Orient with the foul plague of Western vampirism by putting the bite on Chinese vampire cultist Kah (Shen Chan)

Lee's autobiography (Granada Publishing Ltd./Mayflower Books, London, 1978); first published in the UK by W.H. Allen & Co. Ltd in 1977

PURCHASE WENG'S CHOP
HEHE HEHE HEEE!
OR DIE!!!
WENGSCHOP.COM / WENGSCHOPSTORE.COM

MONSTER!
MONSTER!
MONSTER!
MONSTER!
MONSTER!
July 2014
May 2014
Issue 5
MONSTER! BACK ISSUES ARE WORTH MORE THAN THEIR WEIGHT IN HELL BANK NOTES...
WENGSCHOPSTORE.COM

REVIEWS

SNOWBEAST

Reviewed by John Harrison

USA, 1977. D: Herb Wallerstein

I can still recall being 13 years old and seeing the commercial for the original Australian television screening of **SNOWBEAST**, the familiar network voiceover artist intoning with slow somberness, "Sunday is the night...of the *Snowbeast*". Like the best Monster Kid sucker, I was lured in, hook, line and sinker, and duly found myself plonked in the black beanbag on the lounge room floor, eyes glued to the screen as 8:30 p.m. rolled around that Sunday. No doubt, I would have had my regular small stack of latest *Famous Monsters, Starlog* and *House of Hammer* magazines beside me, to skim through during the commercials.

There's no doubt that **SNOWBEAST** is a direct by-product of the critical and commercial success of Steven Spielberg's **JAWS** (1975, USA), which not only ushered in the era of the modern blockbuster, but helped keep the "nature strikes back" subgenre alive and popular for the next few years, before the sci-fi craze created by **STAR WARS** (1977, USA) moved in on its territory. Unlike the monster movies of the 1950s, these post-**JAWS** creatures weren't created by atomic radiation, mad scientists or some other calamity. They were just naturally dangerous beasts feeding on anyone stupid enough to venture into their territory (though one exception is John Frankenheimer's **PROPHECY** [1979, USA; see my review in *Monster!* #2], which featured a grizzly bear mutated by mercury-contaminated water from the local paper mill).

A made-for-television movie, **SNOWBEAST** takes place at a popular Colorado ski resort, which is just preparing for its busy season when a string of people start disappearing, usually leaving a mess of bloody clothes behind. Though an eyewitness is certain the culprit was a Yeti or Sasquatch, the owner of the resort (Sylvia Sidney) dismisses the claims for fear of losing business, and dispatches her son-in-law Tony (Robert Logan) to take care of the matter quietly. Helping him are the local square-jawed sheriff (Clint Walker), and Gar (Bo Svenson), a former gold medal ski champion now down on his luck and hoping his friend Tony can help him out with a job. Also along for the adventure is Gar's television reporter wife Ellen (Yvette Mimieux), who at one point had had a ro-

Dutch VHS jacket

mance with Tony, creating an interesting dynamic and tension between the three long-time friends. When the snowbeast invades the Snow Carnival Queen ceremony and causes mass panic and hysteria, Gar, Ellen, Tony and the sheriff head out into the woods in a camper van, determined to track down and kill it...

SNOWBEAST differs from the likes of **JAWS** and William Girdler's **GRIZZLY** (1976, USA) in that it is based on a mythical creature rather than a (proven) factual one, but the formula is exactly the same; just toned-down somewhat for television (especially in the boobs and blood departments). The screenplay by Joseph Stefano (who did much better work on Hitchcock's **PSYCHO** [1960, USA] and *The Outer Limits* television series of 1963-65) apes **JAWS** to such an extent that it even features a scene where a couple of the lead characters discuss cutting open a slain grizzly in order to verify that they have got the right beast that's been eating up all the local residents and tourists! And you've gotta love dialogue exchanges like this (delivered with the utmost seriousness, of course):

Sheriff Paraday: *"I understand she was a guest at your ski lodge. I was hoping you could help me identify her."*
Tony Rill: *"I must have seen her* somewhere. *Maybe I'll recognize her when I see her face."*

Sheriff Paraday: *"She doesn't have one."*

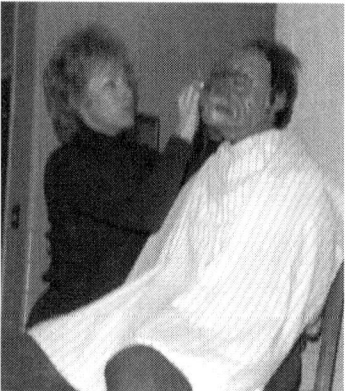

While no great shakes as a monster flick (the creature is rarely shown and the killings all fade to a red screen just as the fun is about to begin), **SNOWBEAST** is still an enjoyable attempt by television to cash-in not only on **JAWS** but on the whole bigfoot/yeti phenomena that was popular during the 1970s (thanks to a plethora of paperback books and magazines, TV specials and faux documentaries like **THE MYSTERIOUS MONSTERS** [1975, USA]). Screenwriter Stefano reportedly used Roger Patterson's 1966 book *Do Abominable Snowmen of America Really Exist?* as the uncredited basis for his research (Patterson, of course, was the person who in 1967 shot the infamous piece of 8mm film supposedly showing Bigfoot trampling through the woods in California). It's a pity the snowbeast itself is not shown more clearly in the film, as it looks to be a pretty impressive suit used to bring the creature to life (with actor Mike London inside it).

The cast of **SNOWBEAST** consists of the usual roster of TV faces and former film stars, including Svenson (a familiar face in '70s exploitation and action cinema), Mimieux (**THE TIME MACHINE** [1960], **JACKSON COUNTY JAIL** [1976, both USA]), Sylvia Sidney and Clint Walker (latter of whom had previously battled killer wildlife in the underrated adventure/western yarn **NIGHT OF THE GRIZZLY** [1966, USA]). Director Herb Wallerstein was an assistant director on William Castle's classic **THE TINGLER** (1959, USA), and spent most of his career directing episodic television shows such as *Star Trek*, *The Brady Bunch*, *Happy Days*, *Petrocelli*, *Wonder Woman* and *The Six Million Dollar Man*.[1] His own ending at the age of 59 could have made for a good TV movie itself: he was bludgeoned to death in 1985 by an illegal alien from El Salvador who had been working as Wallerstein's maid at the time.

I don't recall **SNOWBEAST** ever being repeated on Australian television after its initial airing, though it did appear on VHS over here in the 1980s (under the generic retitling of **BIGFOOT**). It's a title now clearly in the public domain, as it has surfaced on a number of budget DVD labels in the last ten years, usually featuring a pretty grainy print that looks like it was transferred from an old videotape master. The print I viewed before composing this review

---

[1] Albeit not the February 1, 1976 episode of that lattermost show entitled "The Secret of Bigfoot", which featured 7'-tall wrestler André the Giant as the title hairy hominid.

Top: In a behind-the-scenes shot taken on **SNOWBEAST**'s ski resort set in Crested Butte, Colorado in '77, while made-up as the titular horrible hominid, actor Michael J. London snuggles up to supporting actress Jacquie Botts (who played elected "Snow Queen" Betty Jo Blodgett in the film). **Center:** Beast portrayer London gets his face on c/o makeup artist Dee Manges. **Left:** Tie-in paperback for the theatrically released documentary by Sunn Classic Pictures

was the 2009 Alpha Video DVD release, where it was paired with the 1976 pseudo-documentary **THE LEGEND OF BIGFOOT**. In 2011, a similar but unrelated US film titled **SNOW BEAST** was released, directed by Brian Brough and starring former Duke of Hazzard, John Schneider.

SPOOKIES

Reviewed by Eric Messina

USA/Netherlands, 1986.
D: Eugenie "Genie" Joseph

Ad-line: *"They Want Your Blood!"*

Around Halloween time, while searching for something atrocious and laughable in the same vein as 1984's **GHOULIES** (only more fun) to watch, I found **SPOOKIES**, and have to put it out there for the skeptics who might lump this in with duds like **THE BOOGENS** (1981) or **THE WILLIES** (1990): the present film is a definite crowd-pleaser! This monster flick—which has zombies, a "cat boy" and other ghastlies—is so likeable and ridiculous that I had to bring it over to my pal Paul "Sharky" Vandervort's house. He and his lovely girlfriend Steph Fries hold beer- and snack-fueled trashy movie nights on a big screen in their living room. Some of the most astoundingly good times were had there, and I knew this film would impress their guests on Halloween night—I couldn't just bring over something dull or run-of-the-mill, or I'd get banished from their house for good!

SPOOKIES has got some of my favorite elements that make it required viewing for drunks with discerning palettes. It has the brilliant make-up/creature effects of '80s heavy-hitters Jennifer (**TOXIC AVENGER, STREET TRASH**) Aspinall and Gabe (**BRAIN DAMAGE, FRANKENHOOKER**) Bartalos, farting monsters, ventriloquism and authentic Italian Noo Yawkers (*sic*). This film was originally called **TWISTED SOULS** (co-directed by Brendan Faulkner and Thomas Doran) in its unfinished form, which kind of explains its shaky and confusing beginning with a kid hiding out in the forest and running into a sweaty pervert, who gets mauled. I'm glad they abandoned that storyline, because it gets to a point where the film is simultaneously ripping-off both **THE EVIL DEAD** (1981, USA) and **GHOULIES**, yet the finished product is still original...albeit *totally inept*!

It opens with a kid named Billy (played by Alec Nemser), who gets a rotten birthday surprise in a haunted mansion. The boy has a thick New Jersey/York accent, as do most of the actors in this

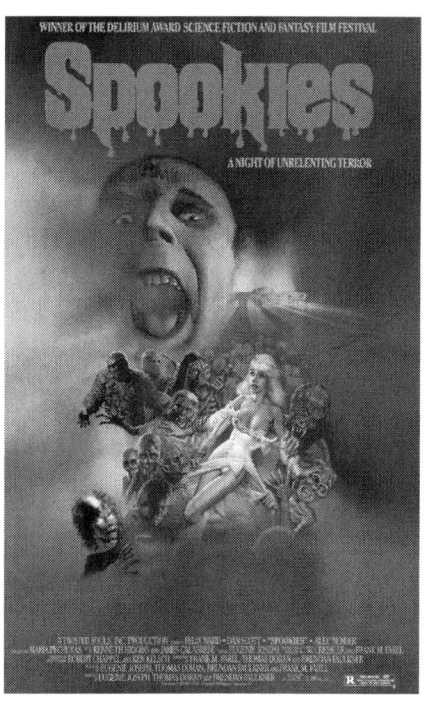

US poster (art by Richard Corben)

film, which gives it an unintentional goofball quality. Billy walks into a dark haunted house and assumes that his parents have planned a party for him. I mean, there are balloons and cake on an empty table; why would they set it in such a cryptic place? Do his parents hate him? Aforementioned "cat boy", who's been lurking in the forest, chases after Billy, then slashes his face to ribbons and buries him alive! That's gotta be the *worst* fucking birthday surprise of all time!

A lispy, wrinkled, ancient-looking Gilbert Gottfried-esque character named Kreon (Felix Ward) hovers over a pretty big-eyed blonde in a coffin. He has an unhealthy fixation with her that is not reciprocated by the female captive, but she is trapped under his evil spell. Meanwhile, a carful of knuckleheads are on their way to party somewhere out in the sticks. All of these characters seem to enjoy partying in a secluded location in the dead of night, which is totally irrational (or totally appropriate for a horror film). The main partiers include Duke, Linda (Duke's redheaded, big-boobed girlfriend), a zany ventriloquist, and four nondescript yuppies. Duke is as intelligent as a bag of hammers, and his odd '80s leotard is unintentionally hysterical (Nick Gionta, the actor who played him, appeared in **STREET TRASH** [1987, USA] in an unassuming gang member role). Rich the

The 40-year-old "teens" find a Ouija board, and immediately try to contact the dead. (I like how Duke takes one look at the board and says, "Hey, don't we need dice or something?"!) Kreon, the owner of the house, seems to have set all the traps that await them, and controls what the Ouija board says. A throbbing vein pops up in the middle of his brain and he demonically possesses a girl named Carol (Lisa Friede). The makeup is pretty impressive for the transformation sequence. *Thriller*-esque zombies start creeping around outside and freak out the dopey kids. As they explore the house, they figure out that there's a horde of monsters about, ready to strike at a moment's notice. Duke and Linda have an oppressive relationship and she seems like a doormat who puts up with his macho bullshit. They end up down in the wine cellar and are attacked by extremely loud-farting "Muck Man" mummies. These flatulent, chunky, decrepit monsters bumble around as wine from the cellar spurts around the room and they fizzle as if someone just tossed an industrial strength Zantac in their direction. When I watched this on YouTube, I thought someone had added the extra gassy sound effects, but according to an interview with the director Genie Joseph, she never intended for them to be included. A British film distributor named Michael Lee forced them to add it into the sound mix, and some of the production team were horrified! Myself, I think it goes along with all the goofiness and fits in perfectly. Had they slanted the film to be entirely serious, it wouldn't have worked, but the toilet humor benefits the clumsy tone. There's one character named Dave (Anthony Valbiro) who looks like Freddie "Boom Boom" Cannon. He minces around, trying to piss-off his snobby girlfriend by drinking booze in front of her. The offspring of Kreon and his bride periodically mug at the camera; they resemble those faces you've seen on Halloween greasepaint makeup ads. I find it odd that the two conceived a child when she was supposedly asleep for thousands of years and wanted nothing to do with him.

My favorite beastie (or "Spookie"), is green and looks like a cross between Mattel's '70s Suckerman toy and Stripe from Joe Dante's **GREMLINS** (1984, USA). It hops on a girl's back and puts its long, gnarled fingers in her mouth.[2] In **SPOOKIES**, the one-sided forced marriage be-

Top & Bottom: In **SPOOKIES**, an alluring Asian woman (played by Soo Paek) transforms into something a lot less easy on the eye. **Center:** Another of the plentiful "old skool" practical special makeup FX seen in the same film

puppeteer (played by Peter Iasillo, Jr.) wears a T-shirt with his and the dummy's face on it, for some odd reason. This actor, along with Joan Ellen Delaney, the actress who played Linda, were both in the abysmal **Ygor AND THE LUNATICS** (1985, USA). Iasillo, Jr. has the most impressive résumé out of the cast, and recently appeared on *Gotham* as a homeless man... *sans* puppet, hopefully!

[2] Credited hereon as "Charlotte Seely", the girl, Adrienne, is played by the uninhibited Charlotte Alexandra, star of Catherine Breillat's controversial "arty" sex drama, **A REAL YOUNG GIRL** (*Une vraie jeune fille*, 1976, France). This English actress—who is definitely one of the more proficient cast members here—also appeared as Thérèse, the "cucumber girl", in the central segment of Walerian Borowczyk's erotic omnibus **IMMORAL TALES** (*Contes immoraux*, 1874, France/Italy/Hungary) –ed.

tween Kreon and his annoyed bride reminds me of the chemistry between Michael Keaton and Winona Ryder in **BEETLEJUICE** (which came out a couple years later, but I doubt they took anything from this film). The demonically-possessed character—who gets mentally enslaved while playing with the Ouija board—reminds me of **THE EVIL DEAD**, and the similar stop-motion melting effects also seem reminiscent of that film. There's a red-eyed grim reaper statue that comes to life and slashes at Duke with a scythe, and it looks like the Spirit Halloween superstore mascot. In a cruelly ironic turn of events, a giant Asian **ALIEN**-type spider latches onto the puppeteer's face and drains him until his head collapses, making him look marionette-like. Kreon is the lamest character in the movie, and his quipping gets old real fast; the actor who played him left the film scene for good and never returned. His undead bride tries to escape, but gets bombarded by endless hordes of zombies and still remains confined by Kreon's mind-control.

This film is very cheesy but incredibly entertaining. I'd say it falls into the category of "monster eye candy", although the actors sort of get in the way of the visuals. There are enough laughs and chaos to keep it bobbing along toward the end… just make sure you're pretty wasted when you watch.

NOTE: For more about this kooky flick, visit http://thedissolve.com/features/oral-history/788-the-strange-saga-of-spookies/

SOULKEEPER

Reviewed by Steve Fenton

USA, 2001. D: Darin James Ferriola

Along with the highly entertaining **TALES FROM THE CRYPT: DEMON KNIGHT** (1995, USA), starring Billy Zane, and the likeable Philippines-shot, earthbound **ALIEN** rip-off **D.N.A.** (1997, USA), starring future "Crow" Mark Dacascos, the present title was one of the very first monster movies I ever purchased on DVD back in the early years of the digital versatile disc medium (I didn't actually "officially" make the switch over to that technology in my movie-watching habits until about the turn of the 21st Century, several years after DVDs first became the new format of choice. For all my stubbornness to make the conversion to discs, however, I could never go back to VHS again now!). As I recall, I picked up **SOULKEEPER** dirt-cheap from a Toronto Blockbuster Video discount bin, having been taken in by the horrendously if irresistibly awful cover artwork (pictured on p.45). Not only does the laughable monster on it—thankfully!—not resemble the one in the movie in anything but the most rudimentary manner, but this "artist's impression" amounts to one of the absolute cheesiest designs of all time, regardless of medium; a dubious honor which assures it at least some place in the history books (and definitely within the pages of this here 'zine). That fact alone ensured I snapped the disc up immediately when I spotted it languishing ignored and dejected amid a pile of

At the climax of **SOULKEEPER**, Kevin Patrick Walls takes pause to give the Magus demon a quick dental check-up while it tries to chew his face off

generic mainstream Hollywood shite, overlooked by everyone...except me! (Well, me and the guy in the user review at the IMDb who said, "The box cover sucks, but the movie rocks"; actually, I have to admit there are a goodly number of more-than-positive reviews for it at said site, so I am not alone in my liking for it.) When I initially popped it in my player, I fully anticipated that the viewing experience would be every bit as cheesy as the cover art, so I wasn't expecting much, but—surprise, surprise!—it greatly exceeded my generally guarded expectations (don't you just *love* it when that happens?!). After my initial viewing, I subsequently watched it a couple more times over a several-year span, but haven't re-watched it since around the mid-2000s; so I figured—what the hey!—I'd not only give it another spin for old times' sake but also pay tribute to it with some coverage here in *Monster!* in hopes of bringing it to the attention of any readers who may have missed it the first time around. I cannot believe that this movie is the better part of 15 years old now! Man, time sure flies, don't it?

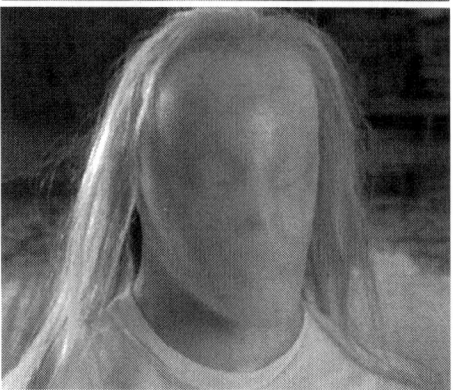

In the prologue, while resurrecting an ancient evil force in the form of diabolical sorcerer Simon Magus (Ed Trotta), a group of bad Bedouin Arabs make a sacrificial offering, giving up their own lives in the process, in best fanatical Islamic tradition. Elsewhere, our youthful heroes—a pair of down-on-their-luck, ne'er-do-well con artists, Corey Mahoney and Terrence Christian (respectively played by Rodney Rowland and Kevin Patrick Walls)—are ever on the sniff for a new moneymaking scheme (i.e., scam), and will take it any way they can get it. But does that mean we dislike the shady bastards? *Nah!* No chance. Quite to the contrary, they're about the most amiable pair of gypsters you could ever hope to get gypped by; and therein lies much of this film's "buddy-buddy" charm. Much like the movie, their friendship is one

---

4 Images from **SOULKEEPER**:- **Top:** A behind-the-scenes shot, taken in the FX workshop, showing a sculpt-in-progress of the major Magus demon. **2nd Pic:** A pair of vampire-like succubi get nasty. **3rd Pic:** Karen Black as psycho psychic Magnificent Martha, "speaking in tongues", so to speak. **Left:** The unsettling "little girl without a face"

non-stop male-bonding ritual...with *monsters!* (Oh yeah, and let's not forget oodles of bodacious human females, too.) While tying one on at a redneck roadhouse deep in the boonies, our rascally unscrupulous heroes meet two sultry young women, one of whom asks them, "Do you believe in the supernatural?" These bedroom-eyed babes succeed in luring the lusty lads to the palatial retreat of an eccentric character who wishes to hire them for a specialized—as in far-from-above-board—assignment. Faking a broad (i.e., technically correct, if overdone) French accent, Brad Dourif appears as this wealthy collector of occult artifacts, name of Pascal, who commissions them—to the tune of $100,000+—to filch something called the Rock of Lazarus for him, so he may add it to his personal collection of fabulous artifacts. As per its name, this mystical relic possesses the power of resurrecting the dead, and is none other than the very same object which recently resurrected that aforementioned malevolent evidently Muslim magician, Magus.

An ex-model now known as a prolific TV actor, the top-billed Rowland—who may or may not (verification, anyone? IMDb doesn't say much about him) be related to Golden Age of Hollywood filmmaker Roy Rowland, director of the classic Dr. Seuss musical fantasy **THE 5,000 FINGERS OF DR. T** (1953, USA), starring Hans Conried in the title part—facially strongly reminded me of a combination of Patrick Swayze and Ray Liotta, while his co-star and onscreen sidekick Walls (best-known for his appearances in Wes Craven's slasher flick **SCREAM** [1996, USA] and Stephen Norrington's vampire actioner **BLADE** [1998, USA]) at times has a pronouncedly detectable Michael J. Fox/Paul Gross quality; indeed, he not only looks like a facial hybrid of those two Canuck actors, but at times—coincidentally enough—even sounds like a combination of both too, and I don't think he's doing it intentionally. Strapping African-American actor Tommy "Tiny" Lister (seen in a plethora of productions, including Luc Besson's cult SF epic **THE FIFTH ELEMENT** [1997, France]) plays Chad, a strong-arm man with criminal leanings who drops such ethnically-slanted put-downs as "greasy Dago" and "drunken Mick" (chalk it up to so-called "reverse" racism!), and in one scene has an unexpected run-in with something-far-from-human in a darkened room (let's just say he gets a real scary surprise when he clicks on his flashlight). As a direct consequence of this nocturnal encounter, Lister's character subsequently becomes inhabited by the spirit of a voracious demon whose tastes run to young men (and not just to *eat* them either, apparently); and in one scene played for inoffensive "homoerotic" humor, Lister is shown propo-sitioning a male street hustler, whom he proceeds to place in forcible confinement for the purposes of doing who-knows-what godawful thing to him. This poor gay guy is later rescued from potentially horrendous sexual molestation by one of our open-minded straight heroes, who obligingly—and surprisingly—enough doesn't make even a single distasteful "queer" joke at the unhappy hooker's expense, nor even a leering double entendre either.

At right around the 60-minute mark, charismatic guest star Robert Davi (seen in the SyFy Channel's **SWAMP SHARK** [2011, USA], among many others) shows up as Mallion, who is seen onscreen for only a limited amount of time during just two sequences, but he makes the most of them. I haven't seen said actor in all that much stuff—the title I just mentioned included—but whenever I do I always find his performances compelling, as here. For instance, he makes for an entertaining "Mexican" *bandido jefe* in Richard Spence's enjoyable made-for-HBO mock-Spaghetti Western **BLIND JUSTICE** (1994, USA), starring Armand Assante as Canaan, a sightless gunslinging antihero modeled after Tony Anthony's title character in Ferdinando Baldi's genuine SW, **BLINDMAN** (*Il pistolero cieco*, 1971, Italy/USA). As for other cast members in the present film, in her one big scene, the late Karen Black really chews on the scenery as a "gypsy" fortune-teller/medium named Magnificent Martha, who levitates off the floor in her chair, rolls her eyeballs up in their sockets so that only the whites show and speaks with Brad Dourif's voice, as well as coming under temporary possession by a transitory demonic entity. In a direct nod to **THE EXORCIST**, lip-synched by a gutturally bestial male speech pattern speaking from beyond this mortal coil, she growls with mucho gusto, "Your mother is here! I just fucked her in the ass! Did you know she likes it in the *a-a-assss*?!" and, purely in the interests of further tasteless comic relief, she/it (*sheee-itttt!*) horks a great glob of faintly greenish gob on our two heroes. No sooner has Rowland then smartassed to Walls, "At least she didn't *puke* on you", than—right on cue—Black (albeit unseen, from out-of-frame) promptly does just that all over the former (adding to his degradation, the same actor later gets guano-dumped on by a big bat in a sewage culvert). Having disappeared for the interim following his single earlier scene, Davi as the mysterious Mr. Mallion subsequently makes his belated reappearance in the 90th minute to lead us into the wrap-up. Possessing the power of levitation, he reveals himself as a guardian angel assigned by you-know-Who (i.e., the *other* "Big G" [and, no, I don't mean Gamera!]) to thwart Magus the devil's emissary from gaining power here on the earthly plane and really fucking our collective shit up big-time.

In a development obviously inspired by Robert Rodriguez's and Quentin Tarantino's **FROM DUSK TILL DAWN** (1996, USA), out in the middle of nowhere hidden behind the deceptive façade of a rundown hotel, the boys find a secret kinky sex club filled with scantily—if by no means scantily enough—clad lesbian vixens, performing tame live sex acts. These sexually predatory females actually prove to be vampiristic, shape-shifting succubi, who seduce our heroes as an overture to sucking out their souls (presumably along with their male essence... but no explicit sexual relations are shown, so don't get your "hopes" up!). With visual effects by Blur Studio, special makeup and creature effects were handled by old hands Robert Kurtzman, Greg Nicotero and Howard Berger (all of whom worked on the aforementioned **FROM DUSK TILL DAWN**, and that lattermost of the three wore the "lesser" demon's costume seen herein). Often in conjunction, between them Kurtzman, Nicotero and Berger have worked on an impressive array of "cult" Hollywood horror/monster titles, including Fred Dekker's **NIGHT OF THE CREEPS** (1986), Jack Sholder's **THE HIDDEN** (1987), Sam Raimi's **EVIL DEAD II** (1987) and **ARMY OF DARKNESS** (1992), Don Coscarelli's **PHANTASM II** and **BUBBA HO-TEP** (2002), Robert Englund's **976-EVIL** (1988), Brian Yuzna's **BRIDE OF RE-ANIMATOR** (1989), Tony Randel's **TICKS** (1993), Clive Barker's **LORD OF ILLUSIONS** (1995), sometime director Kurtzman's own **WISHMASTER**, Mark Pavia's **THE NIGHT FLIER** (both 1997), John Carpenter's **VAMPIRES** (1998) and **GHOSTS OF MARS**

(2001)... and the list literally goes on and on! So by the time they signed on for **SOULKEEPER**, their résumés were in impeccable order, to say the least. The trio's main Magus demon here was a 15-foot-tall animatronic practical FX creation operated by puppeteers, and in addition there was a CG version of the same creature intercut with it, used largely for longshots; as per usual (to my little eye, at least), the practical stuff looks a lot more appealing than the mismatched digital stuff... but that's just me. During one of the only two brief making-of featurettes included with the film's now-vintage 2002 DVD release (by kaBOOM! Entertainment), Ferriola explains about the climactic battle with the main monster, "And of course, what film is complete without having a huge beast blowing up at the end! ... It was just a big foam beast and a 'Terrence' doll". (Spoiler alert! *Oops*... too late. Gee, thanks, man. At least nobody can blame it on me this time.)

Pop singer/actress and future The Asylum schlock monster movie leading lady Debbie Gibson (more recently seen in **MEGA SHARK VS. MECHA SHARK** [2014], **MEGA PYTHON VS. GATOROID** [2011] and **MEGA SHARK VS. GIANT OCTOPUS** [2009, all USA]) puts in a cameo here as "Herself". Lowbrow dudebro humor and purely gratuitous T&A frequently rise to the fore. An amusing sight gag early into the narrative involves our two heroes—both dressed-up as matching Abe Lincolns (complete with Malteser-sized stick-on facial warts)! being pursued across the mock battlefield at a Civil War re-enactment by a troop of enraged, Rebel-yelling Confederates, out for their blood (and it isn't all just acting on the re-enactors' parts, either). In another funny sequence, in order to receive absolution for their innumerable accumulated sins and thus be properly purified prior to embarking on their "holy" mission to trounce evil, Rowland and Walls are jointly intercut in a confessional reeling off their lengthy lists of infractions to a priest, who is left so shocked and spiritually exhausted by everything they tell him that he reaches for the consecrated wine to take a bracing swig afterwards. Providing stylistic counterpoint to all the affable silliness going on, more pretentiously arty touches include a really nicely-composed, out-of-focus shot which at first glance appears to be a stylized human skull. As the camera zooms in closer and focuses on this image however, it is revealed to actually be a still "life" (i.e., death) tableau, central to which is an eyeless woman's corpse. This creatively visualized shot—looking like something right out of an artier Italo *giallo*—doesn't appear to have been engineered completely with CG, and is quite striking, even if it doesn't really serve much of a relevant purpose other than to add further visual interest to an already well-stuffed—some might say overly busy—package.

That said, plot-wise this thing is really all over the map, at times causing the action to appear episodic and disjointed while we hop from one scene to the next virtually willy-nilly. Going off on too many refractory tangents, the labyrinthine screenplay penned by sadly none-too-prolific indie co-producer/director Ferriola strives to be complex but largely registers as simply cluttered and confusing. The script—which includes the memorable impromptu line, "I *piss* on Lawrence Welk!" dropped as a cheap throwaway gag in passing, and that much funnier for it (it's all in the timing, don't you know)—tries to cram in way too much plot and too many characters, and frankly, it's quite the chore trying to make sense of it all. So best you don't even bother trying to put all the disparate parts together too carefully in your head, because, rather like a whole bunch of pieces from several different jigsaw puzzles all randomly jumbled-up in the same box, many of the individual pieces don't fit too well with the others. So instead, rather than worry about fitting them together into any logical sort of pattern, just sit back and enjoy each nonsensical new development as they come at ya. Although, knowing what to expect on this my approximately fourth viewing of the film, I of course wasn't taken by surprise anywhere near as much as I was on my first viewing over a decade ago; but there were a few odd little bits here and there I'd forgotten were in it, so it was nice to have my memory refreshed. But all you unsuspecting **SOULKEEPER** virgins out there (wherever and whoever ye may be) take note: chances are, if you gravitate to this sort of nonsense in any way, shape or form—and why would you have your nose in this here 'zine if you don't?—you're gonna really enjoy having your cherry popped!

Boasting good sets, some well-chosen locations and produced on a quite substantial budget for this sort of modest fare (which was shot on a comparatively short 28-day schedule), maximum production values are evident onscreen throughout, for the most part (give or take some occasional rough edges, which are to be expected in such a modestly-budgeted effort as this). In open homage to Romero's **NOTLD**, a brief if well-staged (B&W) zombie sequence set in a graveyard occurs during a supernatural hallucination experienced by Walls' character. In a similar if at the same time markedly different hallucinatory vision which the character played by Rowland experiences, he—and we—are creeped-out at the sight of a "faceless" (i.e., blank-featured) little girl. This scene, in which said girl slowly turns to "face" the camera, revealing her pallid, featureless visage, reminded me of a similar startling reveal in Takashi Miike's **THE GREAT YOKAI WAR** (妖怪大戦争 / *Yōkai Daisensō*, 2005, Japan). While such creepy unexpected revelations as these are quite commonplace in Asian spooky cinema, I can't help wondering if maybe Miike may have drawn inspiration from **SOULKEEPER**, which might quite likely be the case, but the likelier odds are it was merely a coincidence, and possibly Ferriola got the idea from some older Japanese *kaidan-eiga*. Although it's neither here nor there, it's always interesting conjecturing

Tongue-Lashing: Secondary protagonist Walls gets slurped in **SOULKEEPER**

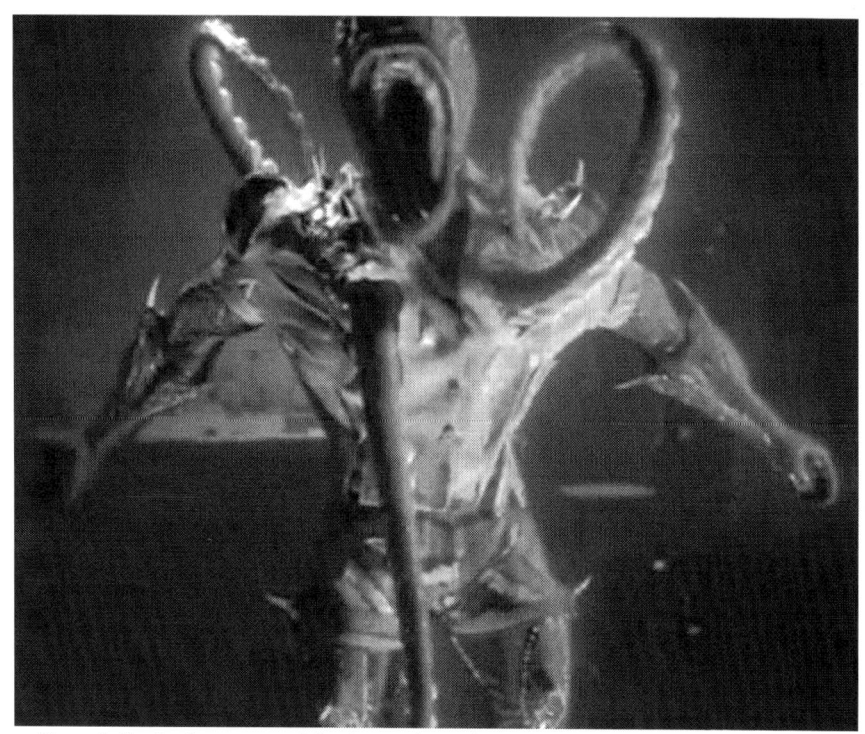

The only fleetingly seen, crudely stop-motion-animated "main monster" of **CREATURES FROM THE ABYSS** resembles some sort of really cheap action figure

at all the many varied sources and influences which filmmakers draw from.

As I alluded to above, there is the odd kinda freaky surprise to be had here and there elsewhere too, and it all adds up to a quite fun package indeed, all-told. For a straight-to-video release—at least I assume it never played any theatrical dates prior to it coming out on DVD, except for maybe at the odd regional horror movie fest (feel free to correct me if I'm wrong)—**SOULKEEPER** amounts to quite the crowd-pleaser. Although I'm sure this flick does have its own fan-base of devoted loyalists, I'm surprised it isn't a lot better-known than it is. Why, until I noticed it on the shelf recently while browsing for something to review here in *M!*, it had quite slipped my mind it even existed. But as soon as I laid eyes on that crap cover described above—which looks like something out of Paul Blaisdell's worst fucking nightmare—I realized what an ideal fit it is.

A really hokey if hard-to-hate anticlimactic romantic twist leads up to the end credits, which are accompanied by a catchy rockin' pop/thrash number by Kevin Saunders Hayes, composer of the film's incidental score. As soon as I heard it, I remembered it from the previous time(s) I watched this, and, much like the film it accompanies, the song is infectious to the ears and stays in your head for, if not days, then at the very least for hours afterward...unlike **SOULKEEPER**, which has embedded itself in my psyche pretty permanently by this point. So give it a friendly spin, won't you? You never know, maybe you'll wind up carrying it around with you always like me, tucked away in some dark corner of your brain.

CREATURES FROM THE ABYSS

(*Creature dagli abissi*, a.k.a. **PLANKTON**)

Reviewed by Greg Goodsell

Italy, 1994.
D: "Al Passeri" (Massimiliano Cerchi)

Ever sit through the latest made-for-home-"entertainment" creature feature and pine for the days before computer-generated imagery? Well, **CREATURES FROM THE ABYSS** has the

48

viewer pining for a little computer-generated imagery! But, we're getting ahead of ourselves...

Five young people—Mike (Clay Rogers), his fiancée Margaret (Sharon Twomey), lunkhead Bobby (Michael Bon) and two nearly naked blonde bimbos, Dorothy and Julie (Laurie Di Palma and Ann Wolf)—go boating in Florida, when they run out of gas. The sea turns stormy, and a man's corpse washes up near their dinghy, whereafter the fornicating five spot a luxury yacht in the distance. Climbing aboard, they find the top floor lavishly decorated in a fashion that would make Caligula retch. Wallpapered in blue tinfoil, a wall sculpture involves a cyclopean fish-maiden who bats her single eye and announces the time with off-color remarks. Yet another sculpture in the men's quarters has a golden satyr with an enormous schlong with a light bulb at the tip. These may sound incidental, but they coalesce later on...

In the lower section of the yacht, the five discover an elaborate marine biology laboratory with lots of mutated fish. They also find a shell-shocked and bloodied scientist who is unable to communicate other than through a series of grunts and squeals, save for this impromptu exchange cooked-up by the dubbing actors to relieve some of the boredom: Bobby: "So, professor, how long have you been fuckin' fish?" Professor: "They were *old* enough!"

These young people do a series of really stupid things—for instance, Bobby rummages through some dangerous chemicals in the laboratory and he sniffs and even *tastes* some—when the true nature of the yacht is revealed: the place is a super-duper scientific marine biology lab out to create mutant fish! The expected things happen, with piranha flying through the air to bite damsels on the neck. The contaminated food they eat causes one bimbo to start upchucking roaches and spiders, Bobby begins to morph into a sea monster...and then the *creatures* begin to show up. And they're about as convincing as the ugly wall sculptures found in the ship's lounge! Two-dimensional, garish and with as much conviction as Play-Doh sculptures. It's the five frat-brats against the monsters until the expected downbeat conclusion.

Director Massimiliano Cerchi is unable to generate any tension, scares or suspense, but it is virtually impossible for him to do so. The characters are attacked by monsters—and then go fix themselves a cocktail in the lounge. Margaret gets bitten on the neck by a flying piranha—and then everybody settles down for a nap. Bob metamorphoses into a hideous monster—and then everyone settles down for a light dinner. These types of projects

1999 Japanese poster for **CREATURES FROM THE ABYSS**

need to keep their momentum. **CREATURES FROM THE ABYSS**' stop-start/stop-start/stop-start structure makes it a real chore to sit through.

For what it's worth, **CREATURES FROM THE ABYSS** remains notorious for two particular scenes. One has Rob mutating into a hideous monster while he has sex with Dorothy, who is either unaware or just doesn't care; a lay is a lay, especially when you're facing imminent death from monster fish mutants! The second notorious feature—an especially gross one—is when both Margaret and Dorothy, after having been contaminated by the twisted marine life, start leaking black caviar from their vaginas! Jesús Franco featured a similar scene in **LORNA THE EXORCIST** (*Les possédées du diable*, 1974, France), with crabs falling from the aperture of Lina Romay, but this scene merely depicted two crabs on a bed comforter with Romay reacting hysterically. In **CREATURES**, the camera lingers on what otherwise would be an expensive gourmet food item spilling from the actress' short-shorts and bikini bottoms! Crude and obvious, one has to admit this is an especially effective bit of "body horror" in an otherwise dismissible film.

Terribly acted with some of the worst dubbing ever, **CREATURES FROM THE ABYSS** is—you've seen this coming from a mile away, haven't you, people?— abjectly *abyss*mal.

Trivia Time: According to some contributors on the IMDb, the dubbed vocals were courtesy of actors C. Thomas Howell and Steve Buscemi… but, like, the IMDb has been incorrect before, righty-o?

ALIEN HUNTER

Reviewed by Christos Mouroukis

USA/Bulgaria, 2003. D: Ron Krauss

The film kicks off with some weird noises on the radio that resemble a vocal track of many a European Black Metal band. We know it's the aliens, silly, because they're in the title!

ALIEN HUNTER is full of strange sights, like this oddball dance-off that appears towards the end of the film.

Julian Rome (James Spader, from Cronenberg's **CRASH** [1996, Canada/UK]) is the hot university professor that every female student lusts after. He receives naughty emails while in class, etc., but these are the least of his problems, as he is now sent for a special assignment to the South Pole. Said assignment involves the scientific investigation of a big-ass object that looks like a gigantic ice rock, but the other scientists on the site believe it is not from this world. They are actually pretty certain that it is alien, because technologically it is much more advanced than what we humans have achieved so far when it comes to what we'll have our whiskey with.

If all that is not enough, the protagonist becomes the object of desire of every female scientist onboard (luckily this doesn't go too far, because it would be off-putting in regards to the interesting story being told here; and yes, it was me who said that!). Another one of his problems is that he is suffering from nightmares—which are visually gorgeous—but this is not explored too much either.

When the object (i.e., the alien one) is opened despite a warning from the aliens, all hell breaks loose (well, almost) and people start dying immediately, presumably due to a fatal virus. These deaths are quite spectacular, and more gruesome ones will follow towards the ending, so if you're into carnage then you'll probably have a good time with this thing.

Now, the best way to describe this film would be… uhh…it's somewhere between John Carpenter's **THE THING** (1982, USA)[3] and Wolfgang Petersen's **DAS BOOT** (1981, West Germany). Obviously it cannot be compared with either of these two masterpieces, but this is not the problem. The flick's main fault is that it is very "1980s"—and I don't mean this in a good way. Notice how the two films I mentioned were both made in the early '80s? If this was made then too, then I would have a totally different point of view about it.

You ask about monsters? Yes, an alien monster does make an appearance, but it looks like it came out of an *X-Files* episode. As a matter of fact, the whole thing looks like an extended *X-Files* episode, especially when Whitehouse, Washington, and a variety of political leaders are involved in endless conspiracy theories that lead nowhere. But I am the kind of guy who has watched the entire 55-disc box-set of *X-Files* and

---

[3] There is some footage used here from Howard Hawks' **THE THING FROM ANOTHER WORLD** (1951, USA), which was also the case with Carpenter's remake.

had a good time while doing so, so I am not qualified to complain.

I didn't see the finale coming. It seems a bit out of place, but it takes you deep into Fantasy-Land, and this sequence would make for great viewing if watched separately; unfortunately, it just didn't fit too well with the rest of the movie. **ALIEN HUNTER** is full of CG, but it is overall so well-shot that you won't mind the gimmicks.

Ron Krauss directed this, and although I haven't seen any of his other films, the Internet tells me that he is usually a producer. The key name here is that of screenwriter J.S. Cardone, who was also behind Nelson McCormick's **THE STEPFATHER** (2009, USA) which was a good remake, and same director McCormick's **PROM NIGHT** (2008, USA/Canada), which was a bad remake, as well as Cardone's own directorial job **WICKED LITTLE THINGS** (2006, USA), which is the horror film with the greatest poster I ever came across for a '00s flick, and so it holds a special place in my collection.

Cardone was also one of the executive producers, and so were Danny Dimbort (the man behind big-bucks flicks like Scorsese's **THE WOLF OF WALL STREET** [2013, USA]), Trevor Short (Sylvester Stallone's **RAMBO** [2008, USA/Germany]) and Avi Lerner (Steven R. Monroe' **I SPIT ON YOUR GRAVE** [2010, USA]). So you do understand that there was no shortage of cash in the making of this? It was reportedly budgeted at around $7,000,000, and loads of it was spent on the aforementioned CGI.

ALIEN APOCALYPSE

Reviewed by Christos Mouroukis

USA, 2005. D: Josh Becker

You rent this film and you think you're in for an "Alien Apocalypse", but guess what, all you get is a short pre-credits narration that lets you know how the aliens (You see? At least they are here!) took over planet Earth. Okay, fair enough, so is this a post-nuke flick? Well, if you consider the outskirts of Bulgaria's forests and valleys to be a viable substitute for atomically-devastated terrain, then yes. This is supposedly set in the post-apocalyptic USA, but it was actually filmed in the Balkans, where film crews are cheap (and strippers are even cheaper…but how would I *know* that?!).

Now that we've established that the aliens have taken over our dear Earth, we're off meeting four NASA scientists that have just landed, after spending 40 years in space frozen in cryogenic fashion. They haven't aged a bit. Two of them die pretty quickly, so we're left with Ivan (Bruce Campbell) and Kelly (Renée O'Connor). To be honest, they don't talk too much like scientists, and they look and act like idiots (yes, including Mr. Campbell, your childhood hero).

Bug-Out! Bruce Campbell and one of the insectoid extraterrestrial invaders of **ALIEN APOCALYPSE**

Renée O'Connor was of course Gabrielle on the *Xena: Warrior Princess* TV series (1995-2001, USA) and, although she has a gorgeous body, her cheeks are a bit chubby (that's always off-putting for me). Still, I think she was way hotter in that show than the title character which was played by Lucy Lawless, who looks too much like Blackie Lawless from W.A.S.P. (the hair-metal band), and that can't be a good thing. Lucy Lawless actually turned down this part whilst doing the **BOOGEYMAN** remake (2005, USA/New Zealand/Germany), so I'm not sure if we should blame her or not.

Back to the show: The aliens keep humans as slaves. There are even some sell-out humans that look like cowboys and work for the aliens, although I never understood why they had to wear fake beards and ridiculous wigs. I guess simply because not all the guards could be aliens, as that would exceed the CGI department's $1 budget.

Soon the lead couple will be captivated in bondage too. Well, they are forced to wear handkerchief gags to keep their mouths shut, and this is indeed offensive, as the movie has great one-liners delivered by all, especially Mr. Campbell. And so much of the dialogue was obviously dubbed in post-production, which adds a surreal element to the experience of watching it.

But I know you are asking about the monsters... well, these alien monsters are really special, to be honest. You see, they look like human-sized green cockroaches. Their favourite food is wood (no pun intended), but they also behead human hostages and swallow their skulls. Oh, and they occasionally eat cut-off fingers, too. So—although they cannot be considered cannibals because they are alien—it is human flesh they crave, thank you very much.

The rural village in which the film is set has the aliens living in a house made of wood, whose door resembles a vagina. How about we start a serious and pretentious psychoanalytic discussion of "*Vagina dentata*" film-studies horse-shit theories about this particular movie? *Nah, let's not!*

The leads try to liberate themselves from captivity, but while Ivan manages to escape the village, Kelly gets captured once again. Ivan goes far away and finds the Freedom Village, which is small place that has not been invaded by the aliens and its villagers live free and have no imperialist tendencies.

Ivan meets an incredibly hot bombshell (I couldn't help staring at her erect nipples all the time), and together they will lead the Rebel Army. Bear in mind that **ARMY OF DARKNESS** (1992, USA) this is not. The producers spent $1,500,000 in the making of this, and it looks like none of the monies made it onscreen. (Those strippers maybe...)

Josh Becker wrote and directed this, and the only other film of his that I have in my collection is **THOU SHALT NOT KILL...EXCEPT** (a.k.a. **STRYKER'S WAR**, 1985, USA), which is a masterpiece, so it wouldn't be fair comparing the two.

Okay, forget those silly discussions about what's good and what's bad. I simply don't care about such definitions. This is entertaining as hell, and you should definitely at least watch it, if not add it to your collection. It was premiered on Sci Fi Channel in early 2005, and received a DVD release shortly afterwards, so by all means hunt that disc down!

CURSE OF EVIL
(邪咒 / *Xie zhou*)

Reviewed by Eric Messina

Hong Kong, 1982. D: Kuei Chih-hung

At times I like to read my own work over at Theater of Guts (*www.theaterofguts.com*), just to refresh my memory on what oddities I should review there at a later date. I've got all sorts of bizarre Hong Kong "Category III", action, and horror to wade through in my quest to see everything disturbing and gruesome that appeared in the *Deep Red* VHS bootleg catalog. In my take on the Shaw Brothers studio effort **BEWITCHED** (蠱 / *Gu*, 1981, HK), also directed by Kuei Chih-hung of the present title, I brought up a film that I meant to watch, but totally forgot about. But once I saw the trailer for **CURSE OF EVIL**, and caught a glimpse of some of those wacky puppets (or schluppets), I knew I had to save it for *Monster!* since it's got some of the most hideously adorable beasts, which deserve to be showcased in all their glory. I've mentioned this director before in the last issue of *Weng's Chop* (#6.5), in my review for **GHOST EYES** (眼鬼 / *Gui yan*, 1974, HK), as the kind of gore-drenched filmmaker whose work is so extreme that you become addicted to that visceral fix and crave more. This time around however, **CURSE OF EVIL** is only *half*-good, and doesn't ever really get all that offensive or mind-blowing. This flick is worth tolerating enough to see those wacky monster hijinks, which are pretty cool. Often when the monsters outshine the actors and storyline it's prime material for this magazine!

In the first two minutes, take cover, because torrential amounts of words and letters are about to slice through your brain like a psychological butter knife (good thing there's a pause button, so you can digest all that info)! The Shi family is celebrating their grandma's 50th birthday party, but everything is shrouded in tragedy, since most of the family has died under mysterious circumstances which involve a "dragon king". At the gathering, another relative dies, and it freaks everyone out. It seems as if no one is safe, and they're afraid who'll drop dead next. The grandma (Wang Lai) believes that a bloody frog is to blame for all the misery. Not a minute goes by before a ghostly invader assaults a poor girl who gets engulfed in flames while trying to kill a chicken. When they inspect her back for third-degree burns, they notice that they've since disappeared.

One cutie named Ms. Ming-ming (Lau Nga-lai) thinks that a ghost is responsible. Another attractive girl named Ms. Yulan, played by Tai Liang-chun, is sitting in the courtyard and almost gets her hand bitten off by the mystical creature known as "The Bloody Frog". This pink amphibian's throat is a huge, undulating, bloated sack, covered in human blood.

Yulan's demented cousin Mr. Xu (Ngaai Fei) is going around trying to hypnotize all the women with a silver medallion that he spins while chanting. The family has an elevator in their house similar to the one used in **GREMLINS** (1984) for the enabled grandma character to get around in. Mr. Xu the horny cousin strikes again—I feel like he would fit in more with the oversexed group from **CHINESE TORTURE CHAMBER STORY**(滿清十大酷刑之楊乃武與小白菜 / *Mun ching sap daai huk ying*, 1994, HK). He ties up a naked girl, and this time uses the medallion to trick her into sleeping with him. The producers of this film must've just watched Zulawski's **POSSESSION** (1981) or B.D. Clark's **GALAXY OF TERROR** (1981) and decided to include a similar horny intergalactic or amorous primordial being. The oversexed demon basically humps Yumie to death, and then slithers down the hall. The wobbly-eyed crea-

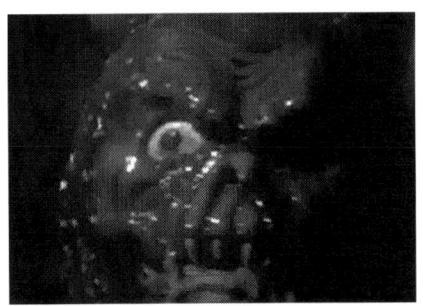

Close-up of a weird catfish monster that attacks folks and gobbles their eyeballs in **CURSE OF EVIL**

ture—which is extremely darkly lit—has horns and flops around as it leaves a trail of pink chunky slime in its wake.

The grandma believes that her family's curse, which was set forth by the Dragon King, has returned to plague them. This turns out to be a ruse for her mental instability that extends to her grandson, and it all comes crashing down toward the end. An inspector wearing an ill-fitting hat (played by Jason Pai Piao) shows up to try and solve the mystery; he suspects someone in the family has brought the monsters back to life.

There's something very unappealing about this Shaw Bros. movie. It's very tedious and the film quality makes everything look beige-colored. The storyline is haphazardly strewn together—I mean, usually with a film from this production company, I'm totally captivated by the onslaught of weirdness and depravity, but **CURSE OF EVIL** just stalls, and its worst crime is that it comes off sort of...*bland*. Yasujiro Ozu, a Japanese director who deals with overbearing family drama, comes to my mind. I've found his work very milquetoast, and had he worked in the horror genre, this might be something he'd come up with. For a Shaw Brothers film, there's a serious lack of gore and frightening creatures here. As the women prepare dinner by dunking a whole chicken in boiling water and chopping up mysterious offal, some unseen hand drags the bloody bits over to a dungeon teeming with frogs and lizards as they munch the shit out of the yummy gizzards.

Yu, another fallen member of the clan, begins to vomit all over the floor and walls. That kind of visceral image won me over in countless stomach-churning sequences during other SB titles, so why is it so uneventful here? I honestly can't explain why. Things get even shittier for the poor unfortunate girl as she lies in bed tied down (for some strange reason), while tons of puppet frogs mangle her face. The plastic-looking amphibians resemble those gumball machine finger puppets you get for a quarter, and are about as menacing. The rapey monster from before apparently hides in the courtyard pool and emerges whenever it feels the need to drown some unsuspecting victim. The tank has tons of leaves floating on the surface; maybe if someone cleaned and maintained it, then a creature wouldn't have such an easy time hiding beneath, waiting to feed on human flesh! The tall beast has lightning-fast reflexes and submerges another family member; this time its "horns" look more like reindeer antlers.

Mr. Yu finally gets what's coming to him (I guess) as a mysterious hand slits his throat and hangs his head on the wall. Let this be a lesson to hypnotists out there learning the trade not to dupe uninterested women into sleeping with them!

If you were like me and sort of yawned throughout the film, prepare to get your eyeballs popped out during a scene involving the horned creature, who strips Qiao totally naked then humps her to death. I mean, sure this is the second time it happened, but the way they treated the rape scene was increasingly more sadistic. The flesh of the creature looks like it's made out of that reddish '70s Wham-O super-elastic bubble plastic material. Sometimes the beast has no legs and slithers around with a giant seahorse-like tail.

CURSE OF EVIL attempts to lull you to sleep for the first part, but the second half starts picking up steam and makes it worth staying awake for. Uncle Quan (Wong Ching-ho), the patriarch of the family, gets butchered in the worst way, down in a frog pit with the little slimy creatures gnawing his cheeks off. Mr. Xu and the last living female relative count skeletons while venturing down into a cobwebbed cavern where they find the grandmother—who's totally out of her gourd—armed with some scissors.

The makeup, which is usually inventive and gruesome, comes off very amateurish and goofy here; something is just "off" about this whole film. Quan shows up later with frog bites on his face and clears up any confusion you may have had about the family legacy and connection to the curse. It's sort of a tearful ending with the last daughter figuring out that she's not related to the evil scissor-wielding grandma, but Quan the ninja-decapitating badass instead. This film has more false endings than **THE LORD OF THE RINGS: THE RETURN OF THE KING** (2003), as they wrap it up with a *Scooby Doo*-style "it was a person behind a mask all along" ending and a warning to be on the lookout for mentally unstable people!

BRAIN 17
(大鉄人１７ / *Daitetsujin Wan-Sebun*)

Reviewed by Steve Fenton

Japan, 1977 [1982]. D: Minoru Yamada

Samples of goofy dialogue from the English dub-job, all randomly strung together willy-nilly, just for laughs: *"...I saw it: a robot monster! ...A robot monster? ...Pilot, shoot that robot! ...I think it was an attack robot, invented by Brain! ...The Brain robot killed my whole family, and my big sister!"*

This heavily-abridged feature, whose original title translates to "*Giant Iron Man 17*", originally saw consumption as a 35-episode kids' series produced by Toei for Japanese TV in 1977. In '82, an American-based outfit called 3B Productions acquired US distribution rights, sloppily recut a few episodes of the original series together seemingly at random (Floyd Ingram is the credited editor) and added new English-dubbed dialogue (as the video-generated titles tell us, this new version was written and directed by one Michael Part and produced by someone calling themselves Bunker Jenkins; a new music score was added by a certain Douglas Lackey). Sometime in the later '80s it was then released to the home video market on domestic North American Beta/VHS cassette by Family Home Entertainment (FHE) under its rather nondescript retitling, **BRAIN 17** (an acronym for "Binary Random Access Integrated Nanolizer" [*sic?*]).

It's always a treat unexpectedly turning up these obscure Japanese TV oddities, especially when they are repackaged into an anglicized format, as here. 20-odd years back, I stumbled across **BRAIN 17** purely by chance while browsing the kiddie section of my friendly neighborhood video emporium. At first glance I assumed it to be more refitted, second-rate SF animé *à la* **CAPTAIN HARLOCK** (キャプテン・ハーロック / *Kyaputen Hārokku*, 1977, Japan) *et al*. To my pleasant surprise, the welcome words "live action" appeared on the video sleeve, and I snapped up the tape for an immediate rental.

A sophisticated super-computer christened Brain 17 ("It's the greatest computer the world has ever seen!" proclaims a cartoonish-voiced narrator) has been shanghaied by curiously Nazi-looking Nipponese terrorists. The leaders of this unscrupulous bunch sport virtually undisguised Gestapo regalia, while their flunkies wear squarehead stormtrooper helmets (incidentally, comical fascistic Orientals are also to be found in Jackie Chan's ultra-goofy

FANTASY MISSION FORCE [迷你特攻隊 / *Min ne te gong-dui*, 1983, Hong Kong]).

A crack military attack unit known as "The Defenders" (alleged peace-keepers despite all their heavy firepower) are quickly dispatched to track down the missing electronic brain and hopefully prevent them nasty quasi-Nazzies from conquering the world. While said Defenders are ostensibly our principal heroes, it is juvenile "Stevie" (presumably listed star Masahiro Kamiya?) who is in actual fact the foremost heroic character. The orphaned Stevie's poor parents are crushed to death in the tremendous landslide caused by a giant robotic creature that erupts from a hillside (in similar fashion to the pointy-beaked extraterrestrial birdbot from **THE MYSTERIANS** (地球防衛軍マーチ / *Chikyū Bōeigun*, 1957, Japan). "I'm afraid there was only one survivor, a small boy, and the rest were all crushed by dirt!" exclaims still another line of hysterical dialogue after the fact.

BRAIN 17's initial daft robot concoction looks something akin to a Republic serial tincanman with a gigantic steamroller welded onto its wrists! This "Roller Robot" (that's what the English dub-job calls it) descends on the nearest available urban sprawl to wreak massive havoc. Its city-flattening spree is interrupted by the advent of a colorful transforming super-robot identified

For the duration of **BRAIN 17**, our boyish hero is able to communicate with his pet robot by means of a hi-tech control helmet. If all this sounds vaguely familiar, you'll perhaps remember that classic boy-and-his-'bot tale *Johnny Sokko and His Flying Robot* (ジャイアントロボ / *Jiyaianto robo*, 1967-68, Japan [see *Monster!* #1]), which was released in an English-dubbed feature version to US television in 1970 by AIP as **VOYAGE INTO SPACE**. The crucial helmet gadget in the present title is later sought by the minions of mean Dr. Hessler, re-programmer of the misappropriated title supercomputer and spearhead of the villainous terrorist organization. Hessler dispatches a pair of beauteous she-android-*cum*-mannequins in hopes of filching Stevie's comptroller headset during a superficially-developed subplot; another involves development by the Defenders of a rival brain machine called "Big Angel". All in all, a lot of plot crammed into a brief amount of time! Indicative of how choppy things are and how loosely they are "tied together", at one point the narrator announces, "Suddenly, one year later", whereupon the action abruptly leaps ahead with a jarring jolt into the next crudely-connected segment of this herky-jerky patch-job. If the show's US re-packagers spent more than a week—if that—patching this thing together, I'd be surprised. The audio track is also a rather odd mix 'n' match/cut 'n' paste affair: for instance, a Japanese jet fighter pilot is dubbed with a drawl *à la* someone from the American Deep South, and gunshot sound FX have the exact same sound as those typically heard in a gazillion Spaghetti Westerns.

To better emphasize its authoritativeness, the super-computer converses with its human thralls in a boomingly stentorian bass voice. Under the guidance of histrionic criminal mastermind Hessler (or is it, more aptly, *Hassler*? The sound of his name seems to vary, but it could just be the muggy audio), Brain 17 engineers the mass mind manipulation of hundreds of convicts incarcerated in international penal institutions, who after being busted out of pokey serve as servile pawns in the evil organization's plot of (*what else?!*) total global conquest. On top of this sketchily explained contingency, the bad brain simultaneously unleashes a deadly "Hurricane Robot": a gigantic spinning propeller-craft not unlike an oversized fan rotor. Also let loose upon humanity is a humongous "Jackhammer Robot" whose piston-pumping method of locomotion causes a violent earthquake. Best of all of these eccentric mechanoid monsters is a big metallic critter (called "Golden Dragon") that spouts fire and slightly resembles some uni-headed Mecha-Ghidrah. Each time, Robot 17 finishes off his latest formidable foe with a

Top: Robot 17 greets his public in **BRAIN 17**. **Center & Above:** The so-called "Hurricane Robot" and "Roller Robot" from the same film, which was actually only a feature hastily slapped together from several episodes of a TV series

by a bright yellow number "17." This robot is the benevolent offshoot of good-computer-gone-bad Brain 17. "Robot 17", as he's logically enough called, strongly resembles the shape-shifting composite megadroid from the early-'90s Bandai Co. *sentai* ("superhero team") show *Fiveman* (地球戦隊ファイブマン / *Chikyū Sentai Faibuman*); but then, I suppose you could say that most such robots in these sorts of shows typically share numerous similarities. Robot 17 was accidentally activated in reel one by young Stevie as he trespassed in the brain-nappers' subterranean hideout.

searing blast and a triumphal booming battle-cry of *"Gravitron!!"*…boy, it sure stirs the emotions, let me tell you.

Unfortunately, **BRAIN 17** doesn't always attain and maintain the manic cartoonish levels of *Johnny Sokko*. But it is a diverting slice of nonsense nonetheless, with enough loud and primary-hued SFX to keep your attention. To add to the infantile hilarity, a kooky-voiced narrator interjects frequent expository voiceovers to propel the plot (and no doubt hopefully more "smoothly" link storylines long since garbled in the hasty reediting process). A disjointed effect results that prevents **BRAIN 17** from ever properly gelling into anything more than a glorified preview trailer for a long-gone foreign TV series. As is also to be expected—see other examples above—**BRAIN 17** is riddled with ludicrously dumbass dubbing (e.g., "Meanwhile the Hurricane Robot continues to ravish [*sic?*] the city!"). An episodic quality is unavoidable on account of its being merely a compilation of reshuffled bits from combined installments of a drastically abbreviated series.

All told, **BRAIN 17** has less soul than some of its ilk (how much depth can you expect from what seems to be spontaneously excerpted episodes spliced into one lamentably compressed 71-minute running time?). The vital robot vs. robot wrestling action is often too hurried by for my liking, but at least there's a sufficient amount of same scattered throughout the show to prevent excessive monotony from setting in.

NOTE: There are virtually innumerable episodes of such shows as this to be found on YouTube, aforementioned *Johnny Sokko* included. An upload of the feature version of **BRAIN 17** is also there, the copy evidently ripped from the FHE videotape source reviewed here.

THE DEMON'S ROOK

Reviewed by Mike T. Lyddon

USA, 2013. D: James Sizemore

Monsters abound in James Sizemore's heartfelt homage to '80s low-budget supernatural horror flicks.

The story concerns a little boy named Roscoe, who strikes up a mystical relationship with Dimwos, a relatively benevolent demon of the underworld. The child descends into the monster's

One of many cool toys associated with the TV show 大鉄人１７ / *Daitetsujin Wan-Sebun* a.k.a. **BRAIN 17**

realm in the nearby woods, only to resurface many years later, fully grown and completely confused. He eventually gets his bearings and realizes he's been chosen to battle the forces of evil which are about to be unleashed upon a small rural town.

THE DEMON'S ROOK is a micro-budget ($75K) feature film Sizemore shot on weekends over a period of two years, and while some of the acting is stiff and the storyline occasionally meanders, the cinematography and practical effects more than make up for the film's shortcomings.

If you love monsters, you *have* to see this film!

Just one of the numerous monstrous entities to be found in **THE DEMON'S ROOK**

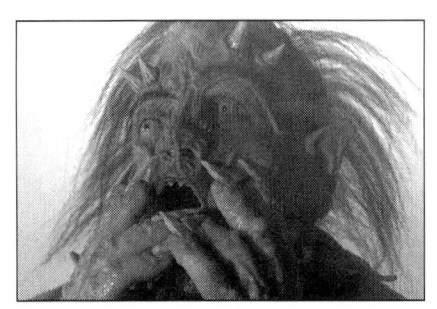

Still another diabolical denizen of **THE DEMON'S ROOK**

The first demon, Dimwos, is perfect in both design and execution, as are the three evil demons which wreak havoc throughout the movie. Folks, these creatures are just plain *wicked*! Like many people, Sizemore is a self-taught makeup artist who learned his craft from books and videos. In true no-budget fashion you have a director who also served as actor, cowriter, producer and special makeup effects artist (a man after my own filmmaking heart).

Not only are the creatures beautifully realized, the zombies in this film are more in-line with Italian director Lucio Fulci's vision. While they can move quickly, they still have that classic rotted, decaying look reminiscent of Fulci's undead and other Italian zombie films of the '70s/'80s.

Then there's the true DIY resourcefulness of Sizemore. During the production of the film, the Sizemore family house in Georgia was virtually destroyed by a tornado. Sizemore turned a terrible event into a great-looking set for one of the key scenes at the beginning of the movie. I mentioned early on that some of the acting was rather stiff, and it's no secret that with micro-budget films such as this you occasionally need to hire amateurs, family and friends, and even crew people to fill certain roles to keep within the budget constraints. That being said, Sizemore's direction of the children at the start of **THE DEMON'S ROOK** is very naturalistic, and every bit as good as child acting you see in bigger-budgeted films. It makes the depiction of growing up in a small rural town rather charming and lyrical, and it certainly struck a chord with my own youth.

Above all, **THE DEMON'S ROOK** was a labor of love for James Sizemore, and that feeling reverberates throughout the film. This is not a taut, gripping horror film, but more so a love letter to European and American monster movies of the '80s, with nods to Fulci, Raimi and other directors of the era. I am sick to undeath of run-of-the-mill zombie movies and cheesy wink-wink send-ups of '80s flicks, and I was pleased to find that **THE DEMON'S ROOK** is a refreshing and genuine homage featuring some of the best-looking supernatural monsters I've seen in a while.

I should mention that while kids play a big part in the beginning of the film, later on it gets rather gory with some nudity which would give it an easy "R" rating equivalent.

THE DEMON'S ROOK is a Tribeca Film release now available on DVD and VOD. It's work every penny of the $3.99 rental fee on Vudu, Amazon or iTunes.

The demon Dimwos and human Roscoe commune in **THE DEMON'S ROOK**, James Sizemore's lovingly put together ode to '80s horror movies

So, what was the one film — the single most startling monster movie — that helped turn you into what you are today? *Monster!* posed that question to our contributors, and here is the first of their reminiscences about…

"MY FIRST TIME!"

I CHOMP YOUR GUTS!

OR, HOW I FELL FOR THE DYNAMIC *OUEVRE* OF LUCIO FULCI

by Eric Messina

The first movie that not only blew my mind, but chomped on my guts and tore out my brain was **ZOMBIE** *(Zombi 2, a.k.a.* **ZOMBIE FLESH EATERS***, 1979, Italy) by Lucio Fulci. It instilled my deep-rooted appreciation for his nauseating mix of gore and scares. At the impressionable age of 9 years old in Long Island, NY at my friend John's house is where I first witnessed the chunkblower to eclipse all others. Even after all these years, Fulci's and Dardano Sacchetti's cryptic tale of voodoo and medical science gone haywire remains one of the most repulsive spectacles of the early '80s.*

As a youngster I watched a lot of inappropriate trash on a Betamax player courtesy of my friend John. At the time, I didn't even have a VCR, and cable wasn't as prominent in every middleclass household during the mid-'80s. In just one afternoon, we watched **HOT DOG…THE MOVIE** (1984), **THE AMITYVILLE HORROR** (1979), **A NIGHTMARE ON ELM STREET** (1984); all films I was forbidden to see at that age. I would never tell my parents about the kind of films that John's mother rented for him (he was a few years younger than me, and they were French). Despite the fact that they weren't accustomed to what uptight Americans were into, his family should've known better than to leave to preteens alone with an onslaught of eye-popping flicks! The mother had an abusive relationship with her son; the entire neighborhood witnessed her beating him on the front lawn. I later found out that they had watched porn together, and she even invented a demonic creature named Gazoo to threaten him so he would do chores. I now wonder if the mother based her demonic coercion on *The Flintstones'* genie character or the Great Garloo toy…but I guess I'll never know. It was a sad situation, and he was the sort of kid who had every **STAR WARS**, He-Man and G.I. Joe playset, plus action figures, because his parents had no idea how to show affection towards him unless it was in the form of materialism. So, there was a whole shit-storm of mental atrocities that caused me to worry about my friend, but I also didn't want to ruin a good thing and have my mom find out I was watching films that were wildly inappropriate for children.

In the sleazy golden era of home video, you couldn't avoid the Wizard Video **ZOMBIE** big-box VHS edition—even if you tried to; it was *everywhere!* The grinning worm-eyed, dirt-caked *papier mâché* mug of zombie cover star Ottaviano Dell'acqua was at the end of every video store shelf in America!

The '80s decade was steeped in hypocrisy and censorship held sway. You had every citizen with a video store account renting demented "Video Nasties" that were banned in the UK. At the time many of these grindhouse staples we all take for granted nowadays were only available in truncated form (most of Argento's catalog were neutered; you could only find the cut **UNSANE** version, never the uncut **TENEBRAE** [1982], or, in the case of Fulci, only **SEVEN DOORS OF DEATH**, **THE BEYOND** (...*E tu vivrai nel terrore! L'aldilà*, 1981, Italy) would remain out of public circulation for years and you could only find the Americanized versions of Italian horror like **DR. BUTCHER, M.D.** (which, oddly enough, I prefer to the **ZOMBIE HOLOCAUST** [1980] version). The first time I watched the uncut version of **THE BEYOND** was through the VHS bootleg catalog of Chas. Balun, which is one of the many reasons why he was so important to the horror community, who demanded to see the originals in all their glory, without the oppressors of film censorship standing in our way.

The public was in denial about these films because they would secretly support them, but also at the same time hypocritically trash them as having zero socially redeeming qualities. It was seriously confusing, and the controversy, of course, helped them sell more videos. The backers always made their money back, and once people became aware that a drugged-up shark fights a zombie in an underwater battle, there was no stopping the public from demanding a copy then! That image has be-

ZOMBIE

© COPYRIGHT 1980 The Jerry Gross Organization

A US lobby still depicting stuntman/actor Ottaviano Dell'Acqua as one of several different zombies he played in the film

come an iconic one (recently and embarrassingly used to sell Windows 7 for your PC, of all things).

MTV had an effect on my brain at the time, and when I first saw Olga Karlatos getting her eyeball pierced and later feasted upon by those walking flowerpots, it for some odd reason reminded me of the Tom Petty video for "Don't Come Around Here No More". Let me explain: the zombies cutting up Olga and shoving her pink wet meaty guts into their dripping maws reminded me of how toward the end of the music video they slice up a woman and eat her like a birthday cake!

From the very first moment that you pop in the video, you hear a gun-blast to the face of a living corpse in a white sheet that emits bone fragments and sinewy chunks, followed by the immortal line delivery by Richard Johnson of "The boat can leave now. Tell the crew," it still sends shivers down my spine. I revisited the film in theaters a few years ago and was slightly disappointed that no one in the San Francisco crowd cheered or laughed at any of the jokes. I myself was howling with laughter at the end, that's loaded with unearthly loud munching and crunching followed by a rain of Molotov cocktails almost on a loop, containing the same shot over and over. That's my favorite aspect of Fulci: he can be clumsy, nonsensical and ridiculous...but I still adore it all of his work.

The scene with Auretta Gay, (who was one of the first naked women I had ever seen in a horror film) totally bewildered me. As I looked at the shimmering blue floating ancient creature moving toward and wrenching off the submerged zombie's arm, I thought, "Am I *really* seeing this? It's just incredible!" The nauseous and captivated feelings just washed over me. I didn't understand the sense of humor yet at a young age, and at the point where the zombie rises from its Conquistador grave and slowly peels Auretta's neck hole open with its teeth, causing it to erupt with a broken-Slurpee-machine amount of artery juice, my friend and I actually ran out of the house and gleefully screamed on the lawn, we were so freaked-out! Those were some images that I remember being unable to scrub from my subconscious the next morning in school, along with a video I saw at John's house of a mystery porn that had a woman inserting bananas into her orifice, while wearing a battle shield and a towel on her head—but that is *another* story... *[Sounds like one for* Weng's Chop, *Eric! –ed.]*

Besides all the H.G. Lewis big-box videos and the Thriller Video ones, **ZOMBIE** has to be one of the most popular of all time. VHS collectors have fetishized big boxes so much now that Charles Band started rereleasing them at astronomically high prices (50 bucks a pop!), because apparently vid-

61

eo junkies will pay that much on eBay! But I think it's shady for someone like Band to prey on the gullible like that. He claims that they just found original big boxes in a warehouse, but according to Paul Zamarilli of *VHS Collector.com*, these are new reprints masquerading as the originals. He compares and contrasts the video boxes—which even have a new Wizard logo on them—to the original copies he's obtained from over the years, and claims they are ripping people off.

It's hard to say whether I miss the dawn of the video era, and I own all the pristine DVD versions of **ZOMBIE** with extra features and commentary by Ian McCulloch. Lucio Fulci's seminal gorefest made a huge impression on my life and converted me as a diehard Italian horror film nerd. That movie has some of the most viscerally impressive undead, which put most other zombie films to shame. There's cross-eyed ones, extremely fat ones and gruesomely pustule-covered ones, oozing grime. When I look at some of the real worms and dripping waxy plaster peeling off the various zombie actors' faces, all I can think about is how effective Giannetto De Rossi's work was, and how the film will continue to stand the test of time.

That said, I lost contact with my friend John after I moved to Florida, and hope he's doing OK… *wherever* he is now.

THE GIANT GILA MONSTER

Reviewed by John Harrison

USA, 1959. D: Ray Kellogg

I'm pretty sure **THE GIANT GILA MONSTER** *wasn't the first monster movie I ever saw, but it's the first one I can remember watching in any great detail. It was one of those movies that, by the time I started getting into monsters in the 1970s, was making regular appearances as the Saturday afternoon TV matinee, and was one of those monster movies that my parents felt was harmless enough to let me watch (trying to talk them into letting me stay up late to watch a Hammer Horror was another thing altogether!).*

Though released on the cusp of the 1960s, **THE GIANT GILA MONSTER** is much closer in tone and style to the low-budget fodder that was playing the bottom of the bill at drive-ins during the mid-1950s. Filmed outside Dallas at the same time as Ray Kellogg's other (more original and effective) 1959 monster flick, **THE KILLER SHREWS**, **THE GIANT GILA MONSTER** combines the monster, juvenile delinquency, hotrod and rock 'n' roll genres to provide a fun slice of B-grade exploitation cinema.

Set in a bleak, desolate rural Texan landscape, **THE KILLER SHREWS** stars Don Sullivan as Chase Winstead, a young mechanic, hotrod enthusiast and all-'round saint. When he isn't working to support his widowed mom and disabled younger sister Missy, he is usually busy guiding the local teens down the straight-and-narrow path, helping the local sheriff do his job for him, and making time with his French girlfriend, Lisa (Lisa Simone, the French entrant in the 1957 Miss Universe competition). He also finds himself dealing with a 70-foot Gila monster: a venomous monster lizard that has started crushing cars and derailing trains in the area, making a tasty meal out of all the passengers. When the creature heads to the local dancehall and interrupts the swinging sock-hop, it's once again up to Chase to save the day, which he does by packing his beloved hotrod with nitroglycerin from the garage where he works and driving the souped-up speedster straight into the Gila monster's welcoming mouth, leaping from the vehicle just before it makes contact.

Co-produced by Dallas drive-in chain owner Gordon McLendon (who plugged this and **THE**

KILLER SHREWS as being the first feature films shot in the area), there's not a whole lot to **THE GIANT GILA MONSTER**. It's the kind of film that people like the *MST3K* group love to send-up, but in reality it doesn't need any help at being amusing and entertaining—it does that quite well on its own. Though Director Ray Kellogg had a long background in special effects before he tried his hand at directing, the monster of the title is just a regular Gila monster, photographed against a model backdrop of toy cars and trainsets, but it has always looked pretty cool and effective to me. When you are a kid and you have imagination, you shouldn't need stunning special effects to draw you into a movie.

I'm guessing Kellogg must have thought Don Sullivan had a big career ahead of him, as much of **THE GIANT GILA MONSTER** is given over to showcasing his talents—his toughness, his tenderness, and his singing voice—as we are treated to him performing a couple of his own compositions throughout the film. In one sequence, he performs the sappy, banjo-driven "Mushroom Song" for his invalid younger sister (*"And the Lord said laugh, children, laugh"*), while another scene shows him belting-out a rocker (*"My baby she swings, she swings whenever I ring!"*) while working on a car in his garage. As good fortune would have it, the car he is working on just happens to belong to popular disc jockey Steamroller Smith (played by real-life KLIF DJ, Ken Knox), who overhears Chase's singing, hands him a business card and before you know it has the kid's voice down on wax, spinning his platter at the sock-hop to the surprised and delighted crowd (at least until the Gila monster sticks his head through the wall and spoils the fun!). Sullivan never went on to a have a huge career, either on film or in the recording studio, but he did appear in a few movies that should be dear to many low-budget monster lovers, including Irvin Berwick's **THE MONSTER OF PIEDRAS BLANCAS** (1959, USA [see *Monster!* #'s 2 and 5]) and Jerry Warren's **TEENAGE ZOMBIES** (1960, USA). He also had an uncredited role in Edward Dein's **CURSE OF THE UNDEAD** (1959, USA) and appeared in Gene Fowler, Jr.'s great gangster/beatnik flick **THE REBEL SET** later that same year.

Containing more than one head-scratching WTF moment (e.g., a man in a business suit hitchhiking through the desert in the middle of the night, and Chase's sister barely able to walk in her new leg braces, yet mere moments later she is expected to carry her own suitcase out to the car when she is being shuffled off to a sleepover!), **THE GIANT GILA MONSTER** will always have a nostalgic soft spot in my monster-loving black heart.

IT AIN'T LEGEND: MANGLING MATHESON

by Stephen R. Bissette

Diseases of the blood (AIDS in the 1980s and 1990s; Ebola more recently), survivalism, apocalypses, urban blight, catastrophic collapse of city economies, xenophobic dread, torture states, shopping during the apocalypse—it's all marketplace currency of late, culturally, cinematically, politically. As a child of the 1960s, I can only say it has always seemed thus. Everything old is new again; everything presented as "new" seems archaic.

Back in December of 2007, I found myself quite enjoying an opening-weekend afternoon matinee of **I AM LEGEND** for most of its running time, despite growing reservations. For my matinee money, David Slade/Steve Niles/Stuart Beattie/Brian Nelson's feature film adaptation of Steve Niles' and Ben Templesmith's graphic novel *30 Days of Night* (the movie debuted October 19, 2007) easily topped **I AM LEGEND** and just about every other vampire opus that year, for a multitude of reasons.

But I'm here to talk about **I AM LEGEND**: In the end, I was left sitting in the dark theater thinking it's too bad that Richard Matheson's source novel remains in need of a proper adaptation—and that's as true today as it was seven+ years ago—but still, it was a game try, and I enjoyed my time with the movie.

Warner Bros. had been spinning this adaptation/remake for years, arguably decades. During its turbulent development history, the project was linked at various points with Ridley Scott, Paul Verhoeven and the California Governor Arnold Schwarzenegger. We ended up with Will Smith as scientist Robert Neville, adrift in Manhattan, on his lonesome save for his trusty companion Sam (short for Samantha, a personable German Shepherd played by *two* dogs; one named Kona, which I find amusing as an old *Kona, Monarch of Monster Isle* comicbook fan) and a horde of daylight-shunning vampires. As with all end-of-the-world urban epics, large or small, since Arch Oboler's **FIVE** (1951, USA) and the first half-hour of Ranald MacDougall's **THE WORLD, THE FLESH AND THE DEVIL** (1959, USA)—in which Harry Bela-

THE LAST MAN ON EARTH (1964): Vincent Price descends the corpse-strewn steps by the Palazzo della Civiltà Italiana (a.k.a. Palazzo della Civiltà del Lavoro a.k.a. Colosseo Quadrato); classical Italian Fascist architecture, built by the EUR (Esposizione Universale Roma) for a planned celebratory expo that was cancelled by WW2—the project was left unfinished for decades, completed in time for the 1960 Olympics in Rome. The familiar landmark also appeared in Fellini's episode for **BOCCACCIO '70** (1962), Michelangelo Antonioni's **L'ECLISSE** (1962), Bernardo Bertolucci's **THE CONFORMIST** (1980), Dario Argento's **TENEBRE** (1982), and Julie Taymor's adaptation of Shakespeare's **TITUS ANDRONICUS** (1999), and many other movies.

fonte was the lone African-American wandering an eerily vacant Manhattan—it's the first third of **I AM LEGEND** that truly worked.

Given the new state-of-the-art CGI enhancements, **I AM LEGEND**'s vistas of a partially-overgrown, quarantined and utterly desolate NYC were the equal of *any* in cinema. The inclusion of wildlife—an inventive grace note fleshed-out quite nicely in Terry Gilliam's **TWELVE MONKEYS** (1995, USA)—added immeasurably to the proceedings, and propelled portions of the film's first third into evocative extrapolations of the best post-apocalyptic pulp, including the venerable Gold Key/Frank Thorne comics series *The Mighty Samson* of the 1960s and Jack Kirby's *Kamandi, The Last Boy on Earth* of the 1970s. So far, so good: director Francis Lawrence (**CONSTANTINE** [2005, USA/Germany], **WATER FOR ELEPHANTS** [2011], **THE HUNGER GAMES: CATCHING FIRE** [2013], **THE HUNGER GAMES: MOCKINGJAY – PART 1** [2014, all USA]) and credited screenwriters Mark Protosevich and Akiva Goldsman were firing on all cylinders, keeping the pace measured and storytelling (punctuated by Neville's flashbacks to his final moments with his wife and daughter during the evacuation of Manhattan) precise. In all this,

Sandy Kossin cover art for the Bantam paperback edition of *I Am Legend*, published in 1964 as an (unannounced) movie tie-in with the AIP release of **THE LAST MAN ON EARTH** (the back cover text began, "I am the last man on Earth!"). This was the only 1960s edition of Matheson's novel

the synthesis of their creative team—Andrew Lesnie's crisp, expansive cinematography, Wayne Wahrman's editing, and James Newton Howard's score primary among those—was perfectly orchestrated and attuned to the narrative.

Then, the monsters intruded. At this point, the film *should* have soared to a new level, but—*it didn't*. It's as if the writers suddenly misplaced their copy of the novel, or were so intent upon eschewing the misfires of the John and Joyce Corrington script for the previous botched Warner Bros. adaptation (**THE OMEGA MAN** [1971, USA]) that they simply lost their way.

In fact, much of the groundwork was effectively laid: Neville's assumption that the vampires weren't intelligent, his (neatly-staged) abduction of a female vampire elevating her infuriated mate to potential villain status, etc. But Protosevich and Goldsman and whoever else was involved in the multiple stages of development hell this script was spun through dropped the threads they were weaving, and director Lawrence allowed the vacuum to

grow, as if the black-ice staging would keep audiences sufficiently off-kilter to forgive or forget the unraveling narrative (more on this in a moment).

So, I can see why **I AM LEGEND** would pull in the audiences—it opened strong and performed well—but leaves many cold. The setup was a knockout: the blowing of the bridges to quarantine Manhattan remains a resonant nightmare scenario, Smith was a likable hero and gave his all, the premise was as engaging in 2007 as it was when Matheson put pen to paper well over half-a-century ago. But the end result fell short; still, given the reviews **I AM LEGEND** scored in 2007, you'd think the critics were writing about some other movie. The plague-apocalypse scenario, along with **I AM LEGEND**'s kinetics, fast-moving undead and insistent oral imagery (the vampire's jaws stretched like yowling banshees) prompted many myopic critics to write this off as an imitation of Danny Boyle's **28 DAYS LATER...** (2002, UK)—forgetting, of course, that it was Matheson's novel that inspired and predated *all* the zombie apocalypse films of the past five decades, including the grandpappy of 'em all, George Romero's **NIGHT OF THE LIVING DEAD** (1968, USA).

My problem with the film were the vampires: they weren't *characters*. Some movies pull this off: the massive zombie hordes of Marc Forster's **WORLD WAR Z** (2013, USA), for instance, were often depicted as a force of nature *en masse*, convincingly tsunami-like in certain sequences, not having to be anything more than locusts (only one rang a bell for me individually: the "chatterer" in the medical installation during the penultimate act). But the vampires of **I AM LEGEND** were less effective by far: yawning, skittering ciphers, more insect-like than human, but not in an effectively disturbing manner, and certainly not in a way that registered with my perceptions or consciousness. They didn't register as *beings*, much less *characters*. This characterizes many contemporary monster movies: the fashion of this CGI era we're in of creatures sans any semblance of flesh or blood physics often leaves me colder than that shivering hyperventilating female bloodsucker on ice in Neville's basement lab.[1]

As if entranced by the effects—and hoping we would be, too—**I AM LEGEND**'s script and director cultivated this *absence*, this complete lack

---

1 See the fully-loaded Warner DVD and Blu-ray editions of **I AM LEGEND** for a glimpse of early vampire character/makeup designs that were ultimately scrapped in favor of the all-CGI creatures in the film. That bonus material is also online at the time of this publication, at:
https://www.youtube.com/watch?v=j22RthvabUM and at https://www.youtube.com/watch?v=cY_MYfueEOs

Ben (Duane Jones) vs. The Living Dead: Matheson's novel was the wellspring for the definitive 1960s siege horror classic **NIGHT OF THE LIVING DEAD** (1968)

of characterization of its primary menace, despite the fact that *the necessary elements were in all place.* Consider:

* The trap sprung on Neville demonstrating how wrong he was in his assumption that the infected had lost cognitive ability;
* The assertion of lead "villain" status upon the male mate to the female Neville was ruthlessly experimenting upon, who (one reasonably assumed, though the film never confronted the plot point) was simply intent upon rescuing his partner from Neville's "House of Pain" (to apply that venerable H.G. Wells moniker here), eventually leading a literal army of his infected kind to do so;
* The final act's buildup, in which Neville had what the lead vampire might consider a "surrogate mate" now in tow, and which still had all the essential narrative components in place sufficient to:
* —culminate in a climactic confrontation with Neville in the basement lab, involving both captive female partners—and where, I kept hoping, *some* articulation of the unspoken role Neville had assumed (he was a monster to the vampires, conducting Nazi-like experiments on the infected) would unfold;
* In which the impressive rescue mission Neville's vampire nemesis had mounted would be acknowledged as a *rescue* mission;
* In which *some* meaningful play, or action, or dialogue between Neville and the vampire leader would ensue;
* In which the *context* for Neville—for the vampire society, for Matheson's final line of the novel and for the film's *title*—would at last be asserted, restored, or simply *used* with some emotional impact.

But, no. The nameless vampire master just kept slamming his fucking self against the glass wall, howling, and we were thrust into a dim echo of **THE OMEGA MAN**'s ending. Neville's status as the feared Josef Mengele of the vampire society was only obliquely acknowledged (via a fleeting dialogue exchange when photos of all the failed experiments were revealed), and nothing but *nothing* came of all these narrative points which had become glaring chasms by the fiery finale.[2]

[An aside about **I AM LEGEND**'s coda, set in Bethel, VT—a real Vermont town, nestled in hilly country at the edge of the Green Mountains, just

---

[2] Also see the fully-loaded Warner DVD and Blu-ray editions of **I AM LEGEND** bonus material to see the original, superior ending ("alternate ending") that was scrapped; it's also at the time of this publication online at *https://www.youtube.com/watch?v=kPSk30qzgFs*

Robert Morgan (Vincent Price) vs. the Vampires: Five years before **NIGHT OF THE LIVING DEAD**, the first authorized (if disowned) adaptation of Matheson's novel set the stage for what George Romero and his creative partners would soon sear into the collective memories of generations to follow—but it all began with Matheson's novel

off I-89 about mid-state—which was also laughable to we locals. The aerial shot introducing the coda revealed a perfectly flat autumn-colored woodland, leading to the final shot of a military-fortified Bethel; this footage was actually shot in and around West Amwell, New Jersey, and it looked it. West Amwell, NJ Town Clerk Lora Olsen confirmed this in an email to me on December 29th, 2007: "...the **I AM LEGEND** film crews were in Mt. Airy for a couple days in early November [2007]". *Yow!* Early November shoot for a film released in December; this production was clearly a pressure cooker, or the coda was a last-minute decision. Lora concluded, "The road from the village to the high school (Mt. Airy-Harbourton Road) was closed—a distance of about 1½ miles—during the day". Thanks, Lora!]

Mind you, this wasn't me aching for a narrative that wasn't there—this was me yearning for the film *to tell its own story, the story the film itself was presenting* without successfully articulating even its *explicit* components.

This is sadly typical of major studio genre films today.

Seasoned vet monster designer Patrick Tatopoulis and his firm, Tatopoulos Design Studios (working within tight deadlines with Sony Pictures Imageworks and Gentle Giant Studios), concocted the all-CGI vampires. Reportedly built upon the key design for the lead vampire (the "alpha male"), the infected—with their veined, marbled skin, extended limbs and somewhat silly stretchy jaws—may have satisfied video gamers, but left this then-52-year-old monster movie fan duly unimpressed. Initially, the infected were to be embodied by live-action performers sporting prosthetic makeup effects, enhanced by selected computer-generated effects; this worked beautifully in the aforementioned **30 DAYS OF NIGHT**, where actor Danny Huston's lead vampire grounded that entire film with a remarkable presence. But of course, that feature also benefited from a stronger script and focus on characterization, which is what in the end foiled **I AM LEGEND**.

The single scariest shot of the movie remains a flashlight-lit glimpse of a pack of the grub-skinned revenants with their backs to Smith (and us) in an otherwise pitch-black interior, preoccupied with feeding on a deer carcass they've snatched. This, the first look we're given of the Manhattan minions of the undead, worked like a charm, though it was immediately defused by—well, *never mind*. That shot was and is a goose-pimple-inducing honey. I also dug the infected canines that figured in the first turning-of-the-tables between Neville and the nominal, unnamed undead nemesis, who really *should* have clicked as a character instead of just a gargoyle.

After that, alas, the computer-game vampire imagery took over, and seemed to infect the whole production with a progressive dumbing-down of what was best about, and possible for, the film up to that point. Let's put it this way: though the "alpha female" Neville experimented upon has *far* more screen time than either the writhing female half-zombie of Dan O'Bannon's **THE RETURN OF THE LIVING DEAD** (1985, USA) or the emaciated vampire-astronaut-on-a-slab in Tobe Hooper's **LIFEFORCE** (1985, USA/UK [see *Monster!* #12])—both animatronic puppets—the **I AM LEGEND** vampire wasn't allowed *any* bond with the audience. She was just a hyperventilating, screeching "thing"—we saw her as Neville saw her, and the movie never transcended that objectifying lack of empathy. In this, **I AM LEGEND** sadly reflected one mortifying reality of 21st Century America to date: America as torture state, objectifying our enemies so completely that even the December 2014 revelations of the extent (and utter failure) of the CIA torture program ordered after 9/11 found countless Facebook exchanges in which average citizens casually, even boastfully, showed no remorse, and in fact supported the torture state we're in. It may have been (and remains) an accurate mirror of American insensitivity and indifference; as a component of the film, it dramatically neuters the narrative.

This was emblematic of the paucity of imagination that undid the film: by failing to empathize in *any* way with its monsters (again, in every way **30 DAYS OF NIGHT** remains its superior in this department), the film paradoxically cut itself off from Neville at the very point we should have been arriving at revelations about *his* character. By the end, any relevance or resonance remaining from Matheson's source material had evaporated, the Bob Marley music and new context for the titular last line was as adrift as Neville was in the

Robert Neville (Will Smith) and Sam a.k.a. Samantha the dog (played by Abbey and Kona), taking it to the streets in **I AM LEGEND** (2007)

mesmerizing opening.

—

With their usual zealous opportunism, Asylum beat Warner's **I AM LEGEND** to its own opening date by unleashing **I AM OMEGA** (2007, USA) on DVD *a full month* before **I AM LEGEND** debuted. Dig it: this meant that even as Warner crews were rush-filming the new **I AM LEGEND** "Bethel VT" coda in New Jersey, the Asylum DVDs were being manufactured and moving into distribution warehouses. Never late to their own

Robert Neville (Charlton Heston) preparing to be torch-ured in the first of his crucifixion poses as **THE OMEGA MAN** (1971)

Mark Dacascos as Renchard, the titular "last man on Earth" in Asylum's beat-'em-to-the-Red-Box-knockoff, **I AM OMEGA** (2007)

funeral, Asylum has built upon their early 1999-2000 video market entry (with exclusive-to-Hollywood-Video chainstore titles in all genres, including independent/art boutique titles) to habitually beating Roger Corman at his own game. For marketing savvy alone, I tip my hat to the Asylum hucksters time and time again.

I AM OMEGA danced the usual mockbluster dance at the fine edge of copyright violation: how close to an unauthorized adaptation of Matheson's source novel could Asylum get without crossing the line? In this, screenwriter Geoff Meed (cast in the film as the lead survivalist roughneck) and director Griff Furst took stock of all-that-had-come-before, including how absolutely elements of Matheson's novel had been subsumed into the pop aquifers. Their template was essentially what George Romero and John Russo's **NIGHT OF THE LIVING DEAD** made of Matheson's *I Am Legend*, the novel. With the vampire plague supplanted with the generic (post-1968) cannibalistic dead contagion, lone survivor Renchard (Mark Dacascos) found himself not-so-alone and up against not just the hordes of the animalistic undead, but also roving ex-soldiers scavenging the ruins. The movie is a rat's ass spin of Matheson, Russo/Romero, and all that followed ad infinitum, a notch up from 1960s apocalyptic paperback fodder.

Casting Dacascos as the titular "Omega", Renchard, gave an excuse for our hero to strut his martial arts skills less than four minutes into the film, and run through his ritualized exercises six minutes later. Dacascos was a long, long away from the glory days of Christophe Gans' **BROTHERHOOD OF THE WOLF** (*Le pacte des loups*, 2001, France), though (arguably Dacascos' finest hour on the big screen for international audiences). With sketchy efficiency, Meed and Furst covered the backstory in the opening three minutes: furtive landscape shots of a cityscape (including razor wire fencing); furtive nighttime escape of mother and son truncated by an attack from a blood-drooling ghoul, killing the mother and resulting in the boy seized as he stepped out of the temporary protection of the car. It's a memory/dream: Renchard snapped awake, firearm at ready, and we're thrust into the first action set-piece (minutes later, it's confirmed we've seen Renchard's wife and son killed). A fleeting barely-audible explanation for the monstrous night raiders overheard on Renchard's radio provides the rest: biological warfare *blahblahblah* flesh-eating bacteria *staticstaticstatic* and over-and-out. Good enough—this apocalyptic template is so overfamiliar now that we only need sound bites to cobble together an acceptable premise.

No matter that Renchard is hallucinating the broadcast: *so are we all*, every single day, so pervasive is this contemporary mythos. Post-9/11, this scenario is as (or more) culturally hardwired as Chicken Little, the Fox and the Grapes, the origins of Superman and Batman, or the birth of the baby Jesus. No wonder *The Walking Dead*'s creator/writer Robert Kirkman doesn't feel compelled to cut George Romero a royalty check on a monthly basis. It's *everyone's* story, now, and it's all up for grabs: God's Lonely Man Against the World, 21st Century-style, one size fits all. *It's All Legend*.

In short, everything the Italian film industry had already plundered and regurgitated in the 1980s was legally safe turf for further conceptual piracy, so writer Meed and director Furst cut loose within that already-ravaged battlefield. With their protruding spines (sporting cartoony scutes on some, lending them a reptilian component) and lumpen flesh-putty mugs, the nocturnal predatory flesh-eaters were on a par with the 1980s spaghetti horror breed. Slavering gore, these twitchy, toothy pests were feral and fast-moving, dangerously omnipresent but (believably) no match for Renchard, except in their numbers. They aren't characters, but their *lack* of individuality worked here: they were vermin, nothing more.

I dug the first half-hour's no-nonsense, bargain-basement-*sans*-expectations, cut-all-fat-to-bare-the-marrow energy, taking on the mega-budget authorized adaptation it so shamelessly emulated. Then, around the 40-minute mark, it went to shit. Brianna (Jennifer Lee Wiggins) popped up on the laptop, desperate for help; militarist rovers (screenwriter Meed and sidekick Ryan Lloyd) intruded to rope Renchard into service; and the movie declined into an eventual, inevitable *mano-a-mano* between Meed and Dacascos in a junkyard, fighting over Brianna (now, *there's* a writer's conceit!). Still, some original narrative perks spiked the retread: instead of Neville staking vampires by daylight, Renchard's daily route had him planting a network of timed explosives[3] to blow the entire city to kingdom come, and the reason for the survivalists coercing Renchard into doing their will—deep-sixing any hope of redemption for mankind, they *prefer* dog-eat-dog Darwinism—was a neat twist, too. In the end, it was just another direct-to-vid revamp of Roger Corman's already (always) dire **THE LAST WOMAN ON EARTH** (1960, USA), with "zombies": hardly Richard Matheson turf.

Asylum's teams have this down to a precise science, and their marketing department is even sharper. With their usual artful artlessness, **I AM OMEGA** ideally cultivated the desired Red Box-style consumer confusion (with both **I AM LEGEND** and aforementioned **THE OMEGA MAN**) without cuing the Warner Bros. legal department "cease and desist" letters. So successful was the ruse that **I AM OMEGA** is now a staple of the Dollar General $5 multi-title DVD packages. These Asylum movie lifespans perfectly emulate the venerable American-International Pictures (AIP) and New World Pictures longevity-of-titles in the old drive-in theater markets of the 1960s, 1970s and early 1980s. Instead of going from theatrical first-run to second and third runs to triple-bill fodder to dusk-to-dawn show fillers, Asylum titles like **I AM OMEGA** go from the Red Box DVD debut window, into the three-titles-per-pack (Echo Bridge Home Entertainment, #91391, circa 2010, "3 Film Set" co-featured with "Erik Estenberg"'s **MONSTER** [2008, USA; see *Mon-*

ster! #11] and Scott Harper's **AVH: ALIEN VS. HUNTER** [2009, USA]), into the $5 bargain rack 12-title-packs and blowout bin 20-title packs. This happens roughly in as much time as it used to take AIP to relegate once-new exploitation to the bottom of their multiple bills at drive-ins. Now, **I AM OMEGA** can be found in the same Big Lots racks with the Will Smith **I AM LEGEND**...

Nothing is Legend.

Not for long, anyway.

—

There was a time, though, when Richard Matheson's concept was all-new and never-before-seen-or-thought-of.

Matheson's original *I Am Legend* (1954) was the *Robinson Crusoe* (1719) of 1950s post-apocalyptic SF novels, and just as essential a read. While almost all Cold War apocalyptic fiction involved (at least in their final chapters) the cooperative efforts of fellow survivors and/or the coalescing of new communities, Matheson's *I Am Legend* sustained the plight and blight of its lone survivor for the duration, mounting a pragmatic, relentless portrait of that isolation.

Furthermore, the "plague victims" were indeed *vampires*, and nothing but. Matheson's ingenious rationalizations of vampire legend and lore laid out the first believable biological premise for the archetype. No one has done it better since, few have tried.

[Another aside: In fact, it was the invented physiology of *I Am Legend* which Alan Moore adopted wholly for our *Saga of the Swamp Thing* #38-39 "water vampires" two-parter (of which I only penciled part two; both published spring/summer 1985[4]). I have very fond memories of walking on a sunny day with Alan, John Totleben and my then-two-year-old daughter Maia on the road and in the woods around our old Wilmington, VT, Chimney Hill development home during Alan's one and only visit to Vermont, brainstorming that sequel to the Marty Pasko/Tom Yeates vampire village issue earlier in the *Swamp Thing* run. It was Matheson's notion of vampire physiology Alan and I recalled during that walk (as a delighted little Maia Rose took Alan's hand and my own and swung happily between us as we walked and chatted about why staking vampires killed them in *I Am Legend*), and which Alan ultimately used. So, a personal cre-

---

3 Explosions are almost always the kiss of death in Asylum and similar direct-to-DVD action/SF/horror outings, and **I AM OMEGA** is no different. Skirting real ballistics and explosives for sub-par computer-generated "explosions" never works. The movie loses traction during the supposed "destruction" of Renchard's fortress home: the rocket-launcher demolition via a "fiery" CGI burst isn't believable for a second, and all subsequent shots betray that *nothing happened* (no smoke, no fire, no ruins). The clumsy staging and editing of the whole sequence—at one point all three characters are on one side of the fence, the next shot they're inexplicably on the other—loses the viewer, and the movie never recovers. The climactic CGI destruction of Los Angeles is even more risible. But damn, it was in Red Boxes and stores on budget and on time!

4 For more info, see http://www.comicvine.com/the-saga-of-swamp-thing-38-still-waters/4000-261297/

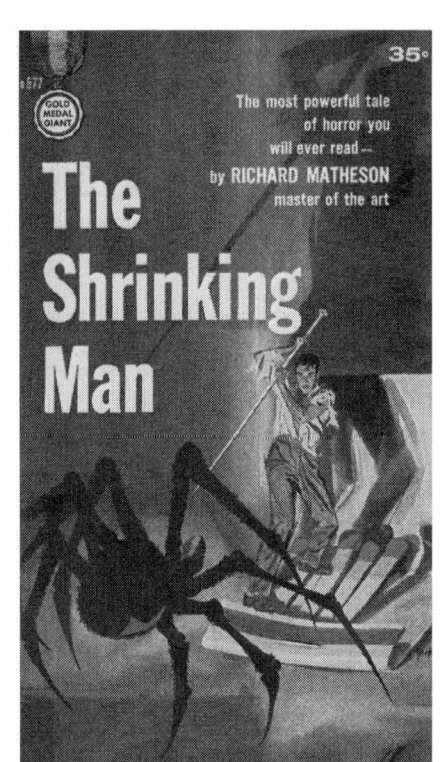

Mitchell Hooks cover art for the original 1956 Gold Medal Books edition of Richard Matheson's instant-classic *The Shrinking Man* (1956). Within a year, the film adaptation **THE INCREDIBLE SHRINKING MAN** (1957) was in theaters, scoring big at the box-office

ative debt to Matheson, duly noted.]

Matheson's hero was Robert Neville, the apparent lone survivor of a pandemic who spent his nights barricaded in his house-as-fortress (as concise a metaphor for America's xenophobic Cold War bunker existence as you'll find in 1954), protected by an abundance of crosses and garlic. Yes, the menace outside was real—the vampires were genuine, not imagined—but the greatest threat to Neville was the relentless loneliness and despair that ate at him. By day, Neville juggled his time between repairing and reinforcing his fortress/home, scientific research into the possible cause (and a potential cure) for the vampirism plague, and methodically scouring the neighborhood for comatose sleeping vampires; once found, he staked them through the heart. Ya, it's a bummer existence, to say the least.

Understandably depressed and filled with remorse, the haunted Neville slogged through the nights of fruitless vampire attacks on his fortress by getting plastered on scotch and cranking up the classical music on his stereo to drown out the sounds of the undead screaming and pounding. Eventually, somewhere amid this, he slept—haunted by memories and dreams of his family's demise and the loss of all he once knew and held dear.

This is as potent in 2014 as it was in 1954.

There were, of course, complications—which I'll leave it to you to discover by reading the novel yourself. Matheson *did* characterize his "monsters" with deft skill that lent the novel the truly mythic scope which has eluded every single film adaptation; only derivative works (not true adaptations) like Romero's aforementioned **NIGHT OF THE LIVING DEAD** and The Spierig Brothers' **DAYBREAKERS** (2009, Australia/USA) capture that mythic power, in their own way. Suffice to say that it was Neville's tenacity in spite of his dire situation and growing despair that made this a terrific novel. Matheson excelled at this kind of intensive, introspective characterization; in this, Neville was a companion to Matheson's *The Shrinking Man*, another Crusoe-like hero exiled via his condition to mounting alienation, loneliness, dread and despair as he shrinks. In *I Am Legend*, Neville dealt with the utter solitude of his fortress because only certain death waited outside. He at times almost succumbed to the inevitable death-wish he could satisfy by simply staying outside after sundown and allowing himself to become, or be fed upon, by the bloodsuckers.

If that doesn't summarize still-contemporary extremist Tea Party/Rightwing/survivalist dread, I don't know what does. Matheson distilled a century of previous end-of-the-world "scientific romances" and science-fiction into a lean, mean, urgently American context; Neville was the justifiably-paranoid lone everyman, alone against a radically changing world. *I Am Legend* became *the* template for all survivalist SF to follow in literature, pulp, and cinema, with or without the vampires. As minimalist rip-offs like **I AM OMEGA** amply prove time and time again, strip everything intelligent away from *I Am Legend*, and you still have an ass-kicking armageddon scenario that rings with surprisingly effective, nightmarish clarity.

Matheson's novels and short stories were and are vividly cinematic. Though it took decades for his excellent *A Stir of Echoes* to reach the screen, Universal-International's success adapting *The Shrinking Man* (as Jack Arnold's **THE INCREDIBLE SHRINKING MAN** [1957, USA]) prompted interest in *I Am Legend* amid the horror revival of the late 1950s, launched largely by the one-two punch of the revolutionary color, eroticized Hammer Films resurrections of Frankenstein (**THE CURSE OF FRANKENSTEIN**, [1957, UK; see p.11]) and Dracula (**DRACULA** [a.k.a. **THE HORROR OF DRACULA**, 1958, UK; see p.25]). In fact, it was Hammer that first optioned and planned an adaptation of Matheson's SF vampire novel, scripted by Matheson. At some point Hammer registered the title "NIGHT CREATURES" for that production (a title later affixed to the US release of Hammer's lively adaptation of Russell Thorndike's 1915 novel *Doctor Syn: A Tale of the Romney Marsh*, which Hammer entitled **CAPTAIN CLEGG** [1963, UK]). Alas, reportedly due to stern objections from the British Board of Film Classification censors (accounts differ as to the particulars), Hammer abandoned their efforts. In short, the BBFC simply wouldn't allow Hammer to make the movie, objecting in principle to the very *premise* of Matheson's novel and screenplay (around the same period, the BBFC similarly shut down Hammer's planned Spanish Inquisition movie, prompting a quick rewrite of an adaptation of Guy Endore's *The Werewolf of Paris* (1933) into the Spain-set **THE CURSE OF THE WEREWOLF** [1961, UK] to make use of the sets which had already been constructed).

Thus, Matheson's script for Hammer made its way—via Hammer honcho Anthony Hinds' sale of the script to producer Robert L. Lippert—through various international production schemes, arriving at the first official adaptation, Ubaldo Ragona's and Sidney Salkow's black-and-white **THE LAST MAN ON EARTH** (*L'ultimo uomo della Terra*, 1964, Italy/USA).[5]

THE LAST MAN ON EARTH has had a sour reputation for generations, undeservedly so. Granted, it falls far, *far* short of the imagined movie Matheson's novel so powerfully evoked in the reader's mind—as has every film adaptation, including the 2007 version—and it was that

---

[5] There are multiple accounts of this troubled production's history, including accounts in many Richard Matheson interviews and articles, but for the sake of brevity we'll steer curious readers to Mark McGee's excellent *Faster and Furiouser: The Revised and Fattened Fable of American-International Pictures* (McFarland, 1996), pp.207-208. For definitive insights into to read the 1957 Matheson script yourself, see *Visions Deferred: Richard Matheson's Censored I Am Legand Screenplay* (Gauntlet Press, 2009, available at http://www.amazon.com/Visions-Deferred-Mathesons-Censored-Screenplay/dp/1934267082/ref=sr_1_19?ie=UTF8&qid=1420500827&sr=8-19&keywords=Richard+Matheson+I+Am+Legend), and/or *Richard Matheson's Censored and Unproduced I Am Legend Screenplay*, both edited by Mark Dawidziak (Gauntlet Press, 2012; available at http://www.amazon.com/Richard-Mathesons-Screenplay-Censored-Unproduced/dp/193426735X/ref=sr_1_6?ie=UTF8&qid=1420500612&sr=8-6&keywords=Richard+Matheson+I+Am+Legend).

Striking abstractions of the male and female form characterized the promo art for the American-International Pictures (AIP) black-and-white SF double-bill of **THE LAST MAN ON EARTH** with the British sleeper, John Krish's **THE UNEARTHLY STRANGER** (UK opening September 1963; US opening April 1964)

73

crashing disappointment that resulted in the immediate genre fan dismissal of the film when it opened. Matheson was understandably unhappy with it himself. The film was based upon his own screenplay, co-credited to William Leicester (and, in Italy, to Furio M. Monetti and Ubaldo Ragona), and Matheson said many unkind things about the movie over the years. He in fact took his name off the credits, supplanting his screenplay byline with "Logan Swanson", Matheson's dismissive moniker of choice for projects he disowned.

Yes, it was a low budget Italian film; yes, the chalky-face makeup and special effects (including a risibly floppy spear in the climactic impalement that really undercut the staging of the climax) were crude. But there was and remains a palpable, inescapable, and irreversible *despair* about the production and the finished film that every single other adaptation fails to approach; a despair that paved the way for **NIGHT OF THE LIVING DEAD** in look and feel and tone and tenor.

THE LAST MAN ON EARTH soon vanished from theatrical play, and Saturday afternoon and late-night TV broadcasts, interrupted by constant commercials, did it no favors. The uncaring pan-and-scan transfer and often murky 16mm, TV and duped prints further degraded the imagery, robbing the film of the clarity and scope of its original widescreen theatrical visuals, making it look like more impoverished a production than it ever was.

Thankfully, widescreen transfers have replaced the videocassette era eyesores, by and large. In 2008, there was a sterling Italian 2-disc DVD edition of **L'ULTIMO UOMO DELLA TERRA** from RHV (Ripley's Home Video) with ample bonus features, offering both the Italian and English-language soundtracks and full 2.35:1 widescreen image, restoring the film to its true glory. It has never looked better.[6] Seen today, especially in the context of the respective failures of the better-funded Warner Bros. adaptations **THE OMEGA MAN** and **I AM LEGEND**, **THE LAST MAN ON EARTH**'s virtues seem self-evident.

Matheson considered Vincent Price badly miscast, and to this day many dismiss Price's performance as too arch, too mannered, but for me he's always rung true enough: it's as if my slightly foppish junior school English teacher or college Theatre professor was the one fellow left standing alone, in every way a more believable average small-town and urban community staple than *Übermensch*-like Heston's "Omega Man" or Dacascos' "Omega." His distraught—if melodramatic—sustained state of depression and loss was if nothing else earnest. Within his range, Price delivered a measured, convincing "everyman" performance that grounded the film, and the screenplay adhered to much of what made Matheson's novel resonate—including, alone of *all* the film adaptations, the true context and impact of the book's final line and its title: "I Am Legend".

There's a studio failure of will that diminishes so many classic science fiction adaptations: a timidity about the *irrevocable change* most key SF novels embrace. This is the failure of two of the three theatrical adaptations of *I Am Legend*—they don't *want* to depict the irreversible cultural shift Matheson's novel charted. Neville became legend because he was literally the last of his breed: *man was no more*. That is clearly *not* the tale Warner Bros. wishes to tell in either studio adaptation. "So *why* adapt the book?" one wonders.

Another case in point: despite all the variations in many media on Robert Heinlein's *The Puppet Masters* (1951), originally published three years before Matheson's *I Am Legend*, none deal with the real subject of Heinlein's novel. This was most glaringly apparent in the "official" feature film adaptation, Stuart Orme's **THE PUPPET MASTERS** (1994, USA); the most *obvious* solution to detecting the presence of the parasitic aliens on a human host—*martial law enforcing full nudity*—had to be avoided at all costs in an "R"-rated major studio feature, though it created an irreconcilable collapse of narrative logic. In Heinlein's original novel—which was restored for its 1990 reprint (replacing chapters Heinlein himself had cut)—this was the inevitable result of the invasion, and nudity became the new social norm! But, no. A similar timidity over the central premise of the source novel undercut the 2007 **I AM LEGEND**, but not **THE LAST MAN ON EARTH**.

Still, there were changes made, only a few due to budgetary constraints. Robert Neville became biochemist Robert Morgan (Vincent Price), and that change in the hero's profession has been carried over to every subsequent adaptation (except **I AM OMEGA**: its hero was a retired special ops soldier). The name change sticks in my noggin: to this day the cry of "*Morgan! Morgan!*" resonates in my head from my teenage viewing of this film on late-night TV. It's Morgan's resurrected vampiric former best friend and fellow scientist Ben Cortman (Giacomo Rossi-Stuart) who shouted this interminably throughout the movie, a line-reading

---

6 At the time of publication, this edition is still available from a number of online retailers, including Amazon; see http://www.amazon.com/LUltimo-Uomo-Della-Terra-Italian/dp/B002RM7WHI/ref=sr_1_1?ie=UTF8&qid=1418530663&s-r=8-1&keywords=L%27ultimo+uomo+della+Terra

rendered monotonously bemusing via dubbing, spicing the otherwise dour atmosphere with inadvertent hilarity (during my Kubert School years and beyond, my late friend Bill Kelley would often begin his often extensive late-night phone calls to me with the hollow-voiced greeting, *"Morgan! Morgan!"*). *"Mooorrrrgannnn!"*: I can still hear that cry![7]

The most frequently-seen still from the film in monster magazines in the 1960s seemed to be the one with Morgan flinching from a reaching vampire hand, and those hands-through-busted-windows-and-open-doors resonated like no other imagery in the movie. It both echoed *and* anticipated genre tropes. The reaching hand was a stage and horror movie staple since the silent era (e.g., serials like *The Clutching Hand* [a.k.a. *The Amazing Exploits of the Clutching Hand*, 1936], "old dark house" plays like *The Bat* and horror movies like **THE CAT AND THE CANARY** [1939], etc). But absolutely central to **THE LAST MAN ON EARTH** was the constant nightly siege, a movie genre staple of westerns more than horror movies at the time. Siege horror was arguably introduced in films like **THE TROLLENBERG TERROR** (a.k.a. **THE CRAWLING EYE**, [see *Monster!* #12]), **FIEND WITHOUT A FACE** (both 1958, UK), and **THE KILLER SHREWS** (1959, USA), and definitively codified by Alfred Hitchcock's **THE BIRDS** (1963, USA). These films all informed Romero's **NIGHT OF THE LIVING DEAD** imagery and staging in ways similar to the night sieges of its precursor, **THE LAST MAN ON EARTH**.

The AIP one-sheet poster for the American release of **THE LAST MAN ON EARTH** played-up its star's iconic face more than the clutching hands, the night sieges, or the vampires, but the film didn't come close to emulating the box office goldmines AIP enjoyed with the Vincent Price/Roger Corman Edgar Allan Poe movies. Due in part to it being in black-and-white when color horror was becoming the new norm, even in drive-in fare, the movie vanished pretty quickly after its first and second runs in the mid-1960s. I've found scant evidence of AIP or regional bookers reviving it in triple features or multiple bills after 1966. It was dumped into one of AIP's lucrative television movie packages to become a fixture of late-night TV broadcast in the 1960s and '70s before becoming a corporate orphan, relegated to the public domain; as such, it quickly became a VHS and DVD market staple, which it remains.

Three Faces Of Fear:- Top: Giacomo Rossi-Stuart as Cortman in **THE LAST MAN ON EARTH** (1964). **Center:** Patrick Tatopoulis-designed CGI lead vampires for **I AM LEGEND** (2007). **Above:** Makeup artist Tara Lang's more reptilian take on the plague-vampires for **I AM OMEGA** (2007)

---

[7] *The Omega Man* has its offscreen lead villain and cult crying out "Neville!" every night, too, but their cries never came close to the resonance of "Morgan!"

Second only to hero Charlton Heston, actor Lincoln Kilpatrick was the most visible cast member in the ads: "The Family" member whose visage was most prominent in all of Warner Bros.' **THE OMEGA MAN** (1971) promotional art and ads

Whatever the leap in technologies, I'll take Giacomo Rossi-Stuart's poorly-dubbed Cortman as nightmare material over the agile Tatopoulis Studio CGI ciphers any day of the week. Rossi-Stuart's role has only gained resonance over the years: since I first heard that cry of "*Morgan!*" on *The Late Show* as a lad, Rossi-Stuart's roles in Mario Bava's **KILL, BABY... KILL!** (*Operazione Paura*, 1966, Italy), Antonio Margheriti SF films and the like made him an iconic figure in the Italian genre films of that era.

I likewise have to acknowledge the potent minimalist chill similarly chalky makeup for the waltzing dead of Herk Harvey's **CARNIVAL OF SOULS** (1962, USA) and Romero's black-and-white flesh-eaters in **NOTLD** have retroactively lent the wan vampires of **THE LAST MAN ON EARTH**. What looked simply amateurish in the early 1960s (echoing the pasty alien-reanimated dead of Edward L. Cahn's lackluster **INVISIBLE INVADERS** [1959, USA] and Phil Tucker's risible **THE CAPE CANAVERAL MONSTERS** [1960, USA]) now carries a weird, corporeal conviction: the haphazard artlessness and *lack* of makeup finesse *enhances* their ghoulishness. Similarly spare makeup effects and "costuming" for **NOTLD** made such desperation look "more real". Despite the often slack staging of key sequences, there's a genuinely disturbing *gravitas*

to the scenes involving Morgan's angst over the resurrection of his dead wife Virginia (Emma Danieli), which, coupled with Cortman's antagonistic role throughout the film, also lends weight to the whole, anticipating the familial autocannibalism so central to the power of Romero's seminal **NOTLD**.

More to the point, however threadbare the production, the script's adherence to the strengths in Matheson's source novel means this film still outstrips the bigger-budget Warner Bros. adaptations. These associative elements, along with the recent laserdisc and DVD letterboxed restorations the film has enjoyed, makes revisiting **THE LAST MAN ON EARTH** a pleasure every time.[8]

—

Which brings me, at last, to the version of Matheson's novel most of you are most familiar with, and likely have the greatest affection for.

Boris Sagal's **THE OMEGA MAN** (1971, USA) became a generational favorite almost immediately upon its release. The movie enjoyed almost

---

[8] For a more comprehensive academic reassessment of **THE LAST MAN ON EARTH**, dig into James Iaccino's Kino Eye essay "The Shadow Destroyer", archived at http://www.kinoeye.org/03/12/iaccino12.php —recommended reading!

constant circulation throughout the decade, popping up in third- and fifth-run drive-in double, triple, and dusk-to-dawn bills all through the 1970s, even as it became TV and cable fodder. Whenever it popped up at local drive-ins, friends who wouldn't go to horror movies with me would call to ask if I was going, and if so, could they join me; I had and have many friends who still love (and quote) the movie. Alas, I don't share the affection, though generationally I should: after all, I saw the film when it first opened (at the Capital Theater in Montpelier, VT, where I later purchased the lobby cards and one-sheet that for a time adorned my Johnson State College dorm room wall and door), and again at least twice at area drive-ins. **THE OMEGA MAN** was unavoidable and inescapable—and it *still* is.

To mainstream tastes, Charlton Heston was a more pleasing, populist reading of the novel's hero—even Matheson preferred him over Price—neatly sliding that 1971 adaptation of Matheson's novel into the complete redefinition of science-fiction-studio-film-as-mutant-action-movie that Heston inadvertently sired. In hindsight, building upon the firm bedrock of George Pal and Byron Haskin's adaptation of Carl Stephenson's short story "Leiningen Versus the Ants" (1938) into **THE NAKED JUNGLE** (1954, USA), Heston-as-star was destined to codify a new breed of "relevant" science-fiction-action cinema with a timely environmental/ecological/sociological slant. Heston gravitated to such fare, which was (in its day) a fairly progressive stance for such a Conservative icon. The weirdly consistent dystopian Heston SF martyr epics are *still* the templates for big-box-office SF/horror/action epics. **PLANET OF THE APES** (1967), **BENEATH THE PLANET OF THE APES** (1969), and **SOYLENT GREEN** (1972, all USA) were thematic and kinetic companions, all three of which I prefer to **THE OMEGA MAN**, which despite repeat visits I have never warmed to. Of them all, **OMEGA MAN** was fueled most by the Messianic associative link with Heston's Moses from Cecil B. DeMille's **THE TEN COMMANDMENTS** (1956, USA)—the plague of blood and the Red Sea parting anticipating the fixation on blood, the (improvised, according to Heston's biography) blatant crucifixion imagery of the grim finale—though all his SF roles embraced and extended Heston's fatalistic string of 1960s self-sacrificing heroes (**EL CID, WILL PENNY**, etc). Who else, of all 1970s Hollywood stars, *could* be trusted to save all mankind? Heston, and everyone associated with **THE OMEGA MAN**, was hyper-aware of this: at one point in the proceedings, one of the child survivors (Jill Giraldi) bluntly asked Colonel Robert Neville/Heston, "Are you *God*?"

In fact, Heston's titular role in **OMEGA MAN** became *the* iconic image of the all-American post-apocalyptic hero, right down to the hardware he carried: square jaw, armed to the teeth, and at ease in or on any vehicle at hand. If for nothing else, this made **THE OMEGA MAN** an iconic pop artifact, and has ensured its lasting stature and entertainment value.

That said, when I caught **THE OMEGA MAN** in its local opening weekend, me and my teenage *compadres* (smartass 16- and 17-year-olds) were laughing at the movie *because* of Heston, and at the lapses that were apparent upon first viewing. Even pre-NRA Presidency, Heston was the epitome of much of what my generation distrusted about institutional pop culture and male role models (in fact, Heston's science-fiction movies played on that distrust as much as they exploited his straight hero status, making him a box office draw *for* the generation gap so pervasive in the 1960s and early 1970s). My high school pal Bill Hunter and I sat through the beginning of the second show just to catch what we were certain we'd seen in the opening ten minutes: sure enough, we counted *four* instances of visible cars moving on the Los Angeles freeways and streets in the background, starting with the *very second shot of the movie*.[9] So much for "The Last Man on Earth" schtick!

Ron Grainer's musical score rubbed us the wrong way—so typical of 1970s studio fare, so anachronistic to the narrative and mood, so reassuring throughout in its flippant TV-movie mode—and the staging of the assault on Neville/Heston as soon as he reached his abode had us cackling, too, even as the immediate presence of hooded cultists further quashed the "last man" gloom the opening minutes worked so hard to evoke. Besides, Neville/Heston already proved himself a one-man self-destructive obstacle to his own survival: shooting-up windows when he glimpsed a figure dashing by the window, but never going to investigate; demolishing his own vehicle due to reckless driving; stealing another car just to park his ass in a movie theater and self-screen **WOODSTOCK** (1970, USA) for the umpteenth time until dusk, the idiot! Besides, we couldn't buy Heston, of all people, digging on Country Joe and the Fish or Arlo Guthrie, since he'd already been shown "grooving" to vapid 8-track rendition of "A Summer Place" while tooling around the abandoned city. His taste in music was reasserted once he was back in his abode—so

---

9 And no, it couldn't be cult members of the plague-infested Family driving these wayward vehicles: it's daytime, they shun the light, and it's a key plot point that the Family refute and in fact destroy any mechanical remnants of the past civilization they so despise.

"Nobody Expects the Spanish Inquisition!" The plague-transformed Luddites played by Lincoln Kilpatrick and Anthony Zerbe lorded over the Family tribunals in **THE OMEGA MAN** (1971)

much for the film's best opening bid to Neville/Heston being "with-it". As one of my pals said, Bugs Bunny-style, "What a *maroon!*"

There's much I enjoy about the film. Trust me, I *do* understand why so many people love the movie. It's more *fun* today than it was in 1971, that's for sure; it hasn't so much aged well, as its anachronism and pretensions have become less distracting or annoying. They're just amusing to me now. Like the Will Smith version, the movie is at its best in its opening minutes, when Heston's supposed isolation is the primary focus. The Los Angeles setting works, and Heston's hero's addiction to private screenings of **WOODSTOCK** (another Warner Bros. film) as his tonic has sweetened with age, just as Bob Marley music fuels Will Smith's Robert Neville. There was a perverse entertainment factor in the movie's Blaxploitation-era elements and inversions. It's no mistake that Rosalind Cash's character looked like 1960s 'Black Power' political activist and writer Angela Davis, or that the infected coven were albinos: instead of Matheson's vampires, Heston was up against race-neutralizing "Whitey-as-contagion" plague victims, black robes and all—if only they'd dared make them more ruthlessly, zealously KKKlan-like, *à la* Spanish Inquisition monks. But that was more than a studio like Warner would countenance.

The fact of the matter was, as the movie unreeled, the albino plague-victim cult never seemed dangerous, not really. Even when they had Neville/Heston at their mercy, they were easily blinded, blundered through, blasted, and eluded. Early on, Matthias and the cult catapulted fireballs onto and into Neville's stronghold. Without breaking a sweat, Neville used fire extinguishers to smother the flames and machine-gunned those manning the catapult, and the assault was abandoned. If he wasn't worried, why should we be? Give me the bleak, dark despair of **THE LAST MAN ON EARTH**, please.

Even the plague-cult's moniker, "The Family", was self-righteous and timely, echoing Charles Manson's murderous commune's self-descriptive name—and remember, Manson believed the murders he ordered would provoke a race war. Here, the "raceless" war of germ warfare Armageddon was a twisted spin on Manson's apocalyptic ravings. Instead of Matheson's vampires, **THE OMEGA MAN**'s contagion rendered all its victims white-skinned, white-haired, white-pupiled ("The Mark"): the Honky Plague.

Debuting a year after (August 1, 1971) the opening of Melvin Van Peebles' **WATERMELON MAN** (May 27, 1970)—in which upscale white man Godfrey Cambridge awoke one morning to find himself transformed into black man Godfrey Cambridge—one would think the "Whitey-as-contagion" would have packed a punch in its day, but the spectacle of Rosalind Cash turning white was far less provocative than that of Heston kissing Cash (pre-transformation). For all this, the movie seemed curiously oblivious to its own subtexts.

Seriously: reduced to the crassest (but still accurate) synopsis, **THE OMEGA MAN** reads like a spin on **WATERMELON MAN**.

Consider this bare-boned distillation:

Lisa (Rosalind Cash) finds/rescues white male Neville (Heston); he rescues her brother (Eric Laneuville) from turning white, so she kisses and then makes love to Neville; then she *goes shopping for an entire day* and *turns white*, joining the Family as they march on Neville's home; the Family kills her brother and then Neville—which, now being white, Lisa sees no problem with.

Huh?? What's *that* all about???

Well, there it is, ladies and gentlemen. Go ahead, tell me I'm wrong.[10]

That's how it played in 1971, for anyone paying attention—and oh, *we* were. A lifetime of *Mad* magazine, Lenny Bruce LPs, and the still-new rush of underground comix made it impossible to see a movie like **THE OMEGA MAN** without paying attention to what it was really about.

Look, Van Peebles and Cambridge knew exactly what *they* were up to with **WATERMELON MAN**; it struck me then and it still does today that **OMEGA MAN** was too blinkered, straight-laced, square, smug, self-important, and somber to hit its own damned grooves. Whitey may have been the new plague, but he still couldn't dance.

Given screenwriters John William Corrington and Joyce Hooper Corrington's considerable academic and writing credentials before scripting **THE OMEGA MAN**, there's nothing to indicate conscious satiric intent—he was a poet, lawyer, college professor and novelist before writing for the screen, she was teaching at Xavier University of Louisiana (from 1968-1979) and earned a doctorate in chemistry, which she claimed in the filmed introduction to the Warner Bros. DVD fueled their decision to embrace bio-warfare as the catalyst for the film's apocalyptic scenario.[11] There's nothing in their other cinema and TV credits to indicate intentional parody subtexts at work.[12] Perhaps sly uncredited script doctor William Peter Blatty (*The Exorcist*) knew what he was doing? We'll never know. Neither savage nor satiric enough, the unabashed spectacle of Heston's iron-jawed messiah complex muscled-out any hint of truly subversive wit onscreen.

To me, **THE OMEGA MAN** embodied such botched potential: of Matheson's novel (willfully dismantled, shorn of its central narrative drive and metaphor), of its cast (even the great John Dierkes—John Huston's "Tall Soldier" of **THE RED BADGE OF COURAGE** [1951, USA], the same year he was among the stranded soldiers facing **THE THING FROM ANOTHER WORLD**—wasted, relegated to a pasty face framed in a cowl), of its own pretensions and premises. 1971 was a great, confrontational, in-your-face, transgressive year for mainstream and independent cinema, but **THE OMEGA MAN** neutered itself even as it unreeled, playing it safe at every turn. By 1971, even the downbeat finale was comfortably

---

operas for US TV (*General Hospital, One Live to Live, Another World*), and they co-created the series *Texas* (1980-82, USA); Joyce later worked as producer and story editor on *The Real World* for MTV.

THE OMEGA MAN (1971) managed to get Matheson's source novel back into print and stay in print in the early 1970s, prominently featuring Charlton Heston and Anthony Zerbe in the distinctive cover art by Mort Künstler

---

10 Revisiting it with friends back in December 2005, this aspect of **THE OMEGA MAN** took on surprisingly, bitterly funny new relevance. As the film blithely cut back to Lisa/Rosalind Cash still shopping in abandoned cobwebbed stores while bad shit happened elsewhere, a female friend laughed, "She's like Condi Rice, shopping for shoes through the end of the world!" True enough! For those with short memories or too young to remember, as Hurricane Katrina rampaged through the Gulf Coast southern states in late August of 2005, Secretary of State Condoleezza Rice was seen spending thousands of dollars on new shoes at 5th Avenue's Ferragamo—and, afterwards, enjoying a live theater performance of *Monty Python's Spamalot*, taking considerable immediate and subsequent public heat for both public *faux pas*. The Ferragamo customer who witnessed Rice's spending spree and dared to express her outrage was removed by security from the store. This wasn't "liberal media" confection: Rice confirmed the event in her autobiography *No Higher Honor: A Memoir of My Years in Washington* (2011), noting her regrets. You can't make this shit up!

11 See Joyce H. Corrington's introduction to **THE OMEGA MAN** in the DVD bonus features; also see http://www.jcorrington.com/authors/

12 The Corringtons scripted Roger Corman's **VON RICHTHOFEN AND BROWN** (1969, USA), **THE OMEGA MAN**, Martin Scorsese's **BOXCAR BERTHA** (1971, USA), Steve Carver's **THE ARENA** (1973, Italy/USA), the sad finale **BATTLE FOR THE PLANET OF THE APES** (1973, USA), and my personal favorite of their films, Curtis Harrington's TV movie **KILLER BEES** (first broadcast February 26, 1974). OK, given the smart subtext of that last film script, maybe they *did* know what they were up to. The Corringtons also were incredibly successful scripting soap

inevitable: Heston's persona demanded it, the audience expected it, and Warner Bros. slickly delivered. Much of **THE OMEGA MAN** was and remains entertaining, in its way, but the bulk of the film's shenanigans seemed increasingly absurdist and silly to me then, and it still do.

Anthony Zerbe's performance as the cowled, albino Matthias, leader of the plague-mutated nightstalkers of **THE OMEGA MAN**, was one of the lasting delights. We meet Matthias in the initial explanatory flashback: he was a TV anchorman for the major Los Angeles station, reporting on the Sino-Russian conflict that unleashed the bio-weaponry which brought civilization to its knees. When next seen and heard in another (flashback) live broadcast excerpt, Matthias' editorial threnody anticipated the cult-leader to come intent on purging any remnant of the culture that consumed itself. These early glimpses of Matthias, well-groomed onscreen and in the studio, echoed **NIGHT OF THE LIVING DEAD** and anticipated Romero's more extensive portrayal of behind-the-scenes media/journalism collapse in **DAWN OF THE DEAD** (1978, Italy/USA). In the immediate context of its day, the infected Matthias was yet another Manson caricature and surrogate—one prominent WB ad campaign even referred to the plague victims as "the strangest sect of all"—but Zerbe brought far more to the role than anything the 2007 **I AM LEGEND** lent its lead menace. Along with Strother Martin and L.Q. Jones, Zerbe was one of the finest character actors of that era, and he lent **THE OMEGA MAN** whatever weight its dramatic core sustained with the understated ferocity of his talents. He alone seemed to inhabit the film as if its mock urgency had some validity. Still, he could only do so much, and was given little to work with.

In the end, Warner Bros. blew it.

White hero, black hero, they just couldn't muster the studio wherewithal to make a proper film version of *I Am Legend*. In the end, both 1971's **THE OMEGA MAN** and 2007's **I AM LEGEND** arrived at *faux*-iconic vials of blood—*savior*'s blood, mind you—and their revisionist corporate studio hope that the implicit "The blood is the life" imagery would supplant the weight of Richard Matheson's original final line and novel title.

Sorry, Warner Bros., but *neither* is legend.

That remains Matheson's accomplishment alone.

He is Legend! —

One final aside: In the spirit of full disclosure, allow me to note that around 1990-91, Steve Niles of Arcane approached me about possibly signing on as artist for a graphic novel adaptation of *I Am Legend*. NJ horror genre book dealer and gentleman extraordinaire Craig Goden personally corresponded with Matheson, urging the author to work with me on this project, but Craig sadly reported back to me that Matheson just didn't care for my work. *C'est la vie*. In any case, there were complicating factors, not least among them the unhappy culmination of the planned Taboo/Arcane Clive Barker *Rawhead Rex* adaptation. In the end, after Niles' Arcane imprint was absorbed by Eclipse Comics, Eclipse published a four-volume adaptation in comics form of *I Am Legend*, scripted by Steve, art by Elman Brown. Steve, bless him, has gone on to great success, including the graphic novel *30 Days of Night*—which is still a far, far better movie than **I AM LEGEND**.

The striking promo art for David Slade's 2007 film adaptation of Steve Niles and Ben Templesmith's graphic novel **30 DAYS OF NIGHT** evoked Templesmith's "splatterific" artwork—and the gory movie versions of Frank Miller's **SIN CITY** (2005, USA) and **300** (2006, USA), both of which had popularized violent graphic novel adaptations at the box-office. The "look" had become codified

©2007, 2015 Stephen R. Bissette, all rights reserved. Revised and update from Myrant, December 29, 2007, archived at *http://srbissette.blogspot.com/2007_12_29_archive.html*

Special thanks to Michael Evans, August Ragone, Tristan Elwell, Greg McEvoy, and Corey Creekmur for help identifying the paperback cover artists.

DINOSAURS ATTACK!™

Remembering the Classic Topps Bubble Gum Card Series
Article & Interview by John Harrison

The first time I laid eyes on Dinosaurs Attack! *(sitting on the glass counter at the now sadly gone Alternate Worlds in Windsor, Melbourne), I instantly felt a connection with those Monster Kids who were older than me, and had experienced that excitement of stumbling upon Topps' infamous series of* Mars Attacks *bubble gum cards in 1962. As a kid, I had bought and collected* Planet of the Apes, **STAR WARS**, **ALIEN** *and* **KISS** *bubble gum cards, and had the odd stack of* Wacky Packages *(or the Australian equivalent), but, as cool as they were, there were none which had any of the kind of hysteria or controversy that surrounded them the way* Mars Attacks *did. Of course, growing-up in late-'Seventies Australia, I had not even heard of* Mars Attacks *at this point in my life. It wasn't until the early 1980s that I would have started reading about* Mars Attacks *and seeing images of the cards, in some of the horror and non-sports cards fanzines that were starting to appear. Learning about the* Mars Attacks *cards and public outcry they attracted made me think of Orson Welles'* War of the Worlds *radio broadcast of 1938, and the mass-hysteria it caused in some parts of the US (I had found a copy of the Welles broadcast on vinyl at the local used bookstore, and had enjoyed the 1975 telemovie about the events, Joseph Sargent's* **THE NIGHT THAT PANICKED AMERICA***).*

I initially bought three packs of *Dinosaurs Attack!* from the comic book store that day, one pack for each different wrapper design I could find, and after taking them home and opening them, assembling them in order and reading the backs and studying the fronts, I found myself laughing harder at any illustrative material than I probably had since I was in college and first started reading *Mad* while stoned. I immediately returned to Alternate Worlds the following day and bought an entire unopened wax counter box from them, 48 packs along with the fold-out store promo poster, and used this to quickly assemble a full set from. I still have it all today, and fortunately the series was produced the way cards should be—in wax packs, with a stick of stale pink gum attached to the top card. Foil packs of cards with no gum just aren't the same! There's a distinct sense of nostalgia and fun, of not taking the whole thing too seriously, in those wax wrappers and the sweet musky scent of that gum.

Issued by the famed Topps company in 1988, *Dinosaurs Attack!* was a series of 55 cards and 11

stickers, which depicted the terrifying carnage wreaked upon the modern world after dinosaurs from the Mesozoic Age are zapped into existence via some kooky space/time experiment which goes haywire. The illustrations on the front of the cards showcased various world landmarks, as well as everyday events like a rock concert and a ball game, as they are trampled, chewed on and destroyed by the giant prehistoric behemoths that are suddenly materializing all over the world. The reverse of each card tells the story of the dinosaur invasion via mock newspaper articles and radio news reports (in much the same way that Welles' *War of the Worlds* radio adaptation went out across America). Fortunately for humanity, a reversal of the space/time experiment literally rips the dinosaurs out of the modern era and back to their own age, taking with them Dr. Elias Thorne, the brilliant young inventor of the TimeScan process which unleashed all the destruction in the first place.

The brainchild of writer/director/designer Gary Gerani, the great appeal of the *Dinosaurs Attack!* series for me was the way it mixed outrageous comic book violence with a simple yet exciting plot and a real wit and flair to the writing. Some of the images and dialogue are as sharp a pop satire of '80s America as anything found in Paul Verhoven's **ROBOCOP** (1987, USA) and Frank Miller's *The Dark Knight Returns* comic book miniseries from 1986. And of course, the artwork is simply stunning—lurid, gaudy, colorful, dynamic and pure pulp. Many images are as grotesquely violent as they are hysterically funny, while others pay tribute to some of the great dinosaur movies of the past (**THE BEAST FROM 20,000 FATHOMS** [1953, USA], **GODZILLA** [ゴジラ / *Gojira*, 1954, Japan], **BEHEMOTH THE SEA MONSTER** [a.k.a. **THE GIANT BEHEMOTH**, 1959, UK; see *Monster!* #12] and **GORGO** [1961, UK] among them). A couple of the cards are just downright disturbing, none more so than #41 ("Entombed!!"), which depicted the bloodcurdling result of a man and a T-Rex accidently being fused together into a sickening hybrid (a nice nod to yet another classic monster movie—Kurt Neumann's **THE FLY** [1958, USA]). There's some nice panoramic battle and outer space canvases, and the appearance of a hideous creature known as The Supreme Monstrosity (!), who shows up towards the end to add a bit of extra bang for your 25 cents. Cards poke fun at MTV, wrestling, fast food and cultural stereotypes (one card depicting the destruction of the Leaning Tower of Pisa shows a middle-aged Italian lady clearly making a *"Mamma mia!"* face at all the chaos going on around her). Amusing little sight gags fill the corners of some cards, such as #5 ("Homeroom Horror"), in which a frog can be seen leaping out of his glass tank, making a quick getaway as an Allosaurus burst into a school science classroom and begins munching on students and the unfortunate substitute teacher.

Top: A baby gets chomped right out of its perambulator in one of the more gratuitously, gleefully distasteful of the 11 stickers included in the *DA!* series. **Above:** One of the more spectacular scenes to be found in the card set. The monstrous dino known as "Ultrasaurus" splits Brooklyn/Staten Island, NY's Verrazano-Narrows Bridge asunder at the height of rush hour!

Not all the cards had a straight newspaper or radio description on their reverse. Some had more creative ways of conveying the story. The reverse of card #9 ("Nupital Nightmare") is designed like a bloodied wedding invitation, while on the back of card #36 ("Comics Con Catastrophe"), the story is told via a series of small comic book panels.

According to an interview with Gerani published in issue #11 of *Model and Toy Collector* magazine (Winter 1988), Earl Norem was the original artist in mind to do the cards, since his classic pulp style was comparable to that of *Mars Attacks* artist Norman Saunders. When Norem was unavailable, the majority of the work went to underground artist Chet Darmstaedter (a.k.a. "XNO"). Earl Norem did eventually contribute his beautifully rich and dynamic art to several cards, as did James Worholla and John Pound (the latter two veterans of Topps' wildly successful *Garbage Pail Kids* series).

A complete rundown of the artists involved in the cards are as follows: Earl Norem did #24 ("London in Flames"), #29 ("Monster in the Museum"), #32 ("Cat Lady's Revenge"), #33 ("Manhattan Island Swamped") and the aforementioned #41 ("Entombed!!"). John Pound did #13 ("Rock Concert Carnage"), #18 ("Tourist Trap"), and #21 ("Fast Food Frenzy"). James Worholla did #8 ("Crushing a Canine"), #40 ("Wrestling Riot"), and #42 ("Lights! Camera! Carnage!"). The remaining 43 paintings —minus the #55 card, whose front contained only a *DA!* text synopsis—were completed by Chet Darmstaedter/XNO. The 11 stickers were contributed by Paul Maurides and Hal Robbins.

I have a lot of favorite cards in this series, but if there was one that I had to choose to best represent *Dinosaurs Attack!*, if there was one card that I could own the original art to, it would be #26, "Coasting To Calamity". Darmstaedter's remarkably bold art of the fictional Gorgosaurus making a meal of some Coney Island rollercoaster passengers is so rich, dynamic and fiendishly grisly, it's up there with the best B-horror movie poster art of the 1950s.

Unfortunately, the *Dinosaurs Attack!* series was only met with moderate success and sales at the time, and a rumored follow-up series never eventuated. A *Dinosaurs Attack!* comic book, published by Eclipse, lasted just a single issue. At one point, there was talk of Tim Burton adapting *Dinosaurs Attack!* into a feature film, but he abandoned it as he supposedly didn't wish to compete with Spielberg's **JURASSIC PARK** (1993, USA), which was in production at the time. Burton, of course, later adapted the *Mars Attacks* cards into a film in 1996, with mixed results (see review following this article).

83

Thankfully, *Dinosaurs Attack!* has developed a loyal cult following over the ensuing years, its art becoming more appreciated and its influence more noticeable over time, and Gerani has recently been able to resurrect the brand via a terrific five-issue comic book adaptation, with art by Herb Trimpe and gorgeous Earl Norem cover paintings, which were published by IDW in 2013. The IDW comic book series, recently collected as a trade paperback, reprinted and followed on directly from the comic book published by Eclipse in 1988. The original card sets themselves can still be found reasonably cheap on eBay, making it easy to obtain and appreciate this wonderful piece of monster pop-art.

GARY GERANI talks DINOSAURS ATTACK! with MONSTER!

Apart from being the brains behind the *Dinosaurs Attack!* cards, Gary Gerani is also a produced screenwriter (**PUMPKINHEAD** [1988, USA], **VAMPIRELLA** [1996, USA]), continues to write comic book scripts, and has authored several books, including the seminal *Fantastic Television* (Harmony Books, 1977). He also appeared as himself in Mark Patrick Carducci's **FLYING SAUCERS OVER HOLLYWOOD: THE 'PLAN 9' COMPANION**, the 1992 American documentary on Ed Wood's notorious opus **PLAN 9 FROM OUTER SPACE** (1959, USA). The character of Dr. Elias Thorne in the *Dinosaurs Attack!* series was modeled on Gerani himself, and it's his photo on the back of card #52 ("The Ultimate Sacrifice").

Monster! *When did the idea of* **Dinosaurs Attack!** *first come to you? Had it always been developed as a gum card set, or did you initially envision it as a comic book, or a low-budget movie?*

Gary Gerani: I had wanted to do a painted sci-fi series ever since I came to work for Topps. In the 1980s, dinosaurs were enjoying sudden popularity with kids, so I suggested a *Mars Attacks*-type card set, but with prehistoric monsters instead of aliens. Much to my surprise, Topps agreed!

M! *How did you sell the original idea to Topps?*

GG: I did a few rough sketches, but basically everyone there understood we'd be doing a *Mars Attacks*-like product again. Art Spiegelman suggested Herb Trimpe for the finished pencils, which would be based on my roughs. Painters XNO (Chet Darmstaedter) and Herb Trimpe took things from there.

M! *How did you settle on the tone of the cards and the story? It's such a wonderful mixture—it pays*

Top: IDW Publishing's 25th Anniversary 2013 reprint of the first issue of Eclipse Comics' proposed 1988 *DA!* 3-parter; however, only #1 ever got published. **Center & Above:** The front and reverse of card #42, which incorporated blatant nods to Godzilla (here re-dubbed "Gadzooka"!)

84

homage to the classic monster movies of the past, yet also satirizes them, and adds a layer of Mad Magazine-*esque* humor to the whole mélange.

GG: *Garbage Pail Kids* was such a success, and the envisioned dino attacks were so extreme, that humor and satire seemed to naturally go along. It just seemed "right"...we were parodying ourselves in addition to the rest of the world this time.

M! *What sort of reception did* **Dinosaurs Attack!** *receive when it was first released? Do you recall Topps receiving any kind of negativity over them? I guess the world had moved on a bit from the hysteria over* **Mars Attacks** *25 years earlier...*

GG: We didn't have too much trouble along those lines. An upset mom called and was transferred to me; I explained that the extreme violence functioned as a grand release for children, that they knew it was all made up because crazy giant monsters were the culprits, not real people. I made comparisons to King Kong stomping on civilians...kids live vicariously through a monster's rampage. It's actually good therapy, according to most psychiatrists.

M! *I gather all the original art for the cards remained the property of Topps? Do you have much in the archives in terms of preliminary sketches, etc., and have Topps ever broached the subject with you of doing a little hardcover book on the* **Dinosaurs Attack!** *cards, like they have done recently with the* **Mars Attacks, Garbage Pail Kids** *and* **Wacky Packages** *series?*

GG: I have the old *Dinosaurs Attack!* "job ticket", along with sketches, designs and Lord knows what else. I'd love to do a *Dinosaurs Attack!* book like the *Mars Attacks* book, and we came close recently. But at the last minute it was decided that the audience wasn't big enough. Maybe someday...

M! *Do you think the cards may have received more attention—or even potentially caused more outrage—if they had hit the market just a few years later, when* JURASSIC PARK *was released and the dinosaur fascination was once again hitting a peak?*

GG: Actually, *Dinosaurs Attack!* was optioned for a movie by Warner Bros. in the late '80s even as the unpublished *Jurassic Park* novel was being offered to the studios. I understand Crichton was a fan of the *Dinosaurs Attack!* cards, and this was part of what inspired him to write *Jurassic Park*. *Dinosaurs Attack!* was optioned a second time, by Tim Burton in the '90s.

M! *It must feel good being able to continue the* **Dinosaurs Attack!** *saga through the pages of the*

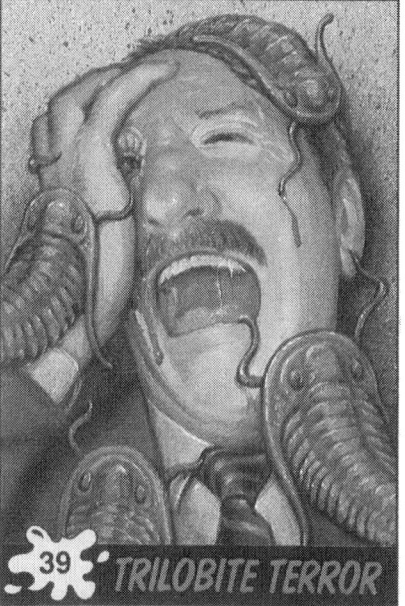

85

love a diorama model kit recreating the "Coasting to Calamity" card! Is a movie option still a possibility? I think **Dinosaurs Attack!** *would have been a perfect vehicle for Paul Verhoeven back in the day.*

GG: Still hoping *Dinosaurs Attack!* becomes a movie someday. Verhoeven would have been perfect back in the '80s, as his **ROBOCOP** did exactly what we did—ultra-violence made palatable due to outrageous satire around the edges. Del Toro would be a fine choice today; **PACIFIC RIM** had something of a *Dinosaurs Attack!* vibe, especially with that early attack on the suspension bridge...

M! *What is your own all-time favorite dinosaur film?*

GG: How about a three-way tie between **BEAST FROM 20,000 FATHOMS, THE GIANT BEHEMOTH** and **GORGO**...director Eugène Lourié's dinosaur trilogy. He manages to do the same story three times, but with different flavors (not to mention different FX artists and techniques). *Bravo, Eugène!*

IDW comic book, and be able to expand on the story and the human characters a little.

GG: Loved expanding the story for comics/graphic novels. That process first began with the now-defunct Eclipse Comics, in the '80s.

M! *Any other* Dinosaurs Attack! *activities on the horizon you may be able to tell us about? I'd a*

Nod to Eugène Lourlé: "Gorgo" buddies up with "Jaws" to snack on the survivors of a sinking ship.

86

MARS ATTACKS!

Reviewed by John Harrison

USA, 1996. D: Tim Burton

If any director of the 1990s was going to attempt a live-action adaptation of the 1962 Topps bubble gum card series *Mars Attacks*, it was going to be Tim Burton. While British director Alex Cox (**REPO MAN** [1984, USA], **SID AND NANCY** [1986, UK]) had tried to get an adaptation off the ground in the 1980s, it took Burton's vision and commercial viability to see the project through to realization, and—on paper, at least—it seemed like a perfect match. Burton was still the young *wunderkind* of American fantasy cinema, having already helmed a series of films which showcased his unique visual eye while also performing strongly at the box-office (spearheaded, of course, by his two *Batman* films). Though Burton's film previous to **MARS ATTACKS!**, the brilliant and gorgeous-looking 1994 B&W biopic **ED WOOD** (1994, USA), starring Johnny Depp in the title role, had been his first commercial failure, it did garner spectacular reviews and a best supporting actor Oscar (for Martin Landau, playing Bela Lugosi), indicating that Burton was just starting to hit his stride as a filmmaker.

It's a puzzle, then, as to why **MARS ATTACKS!** turned out to be such a mixed bag of extremes. As thrilling and gleefully hilarious as it is awkward and disjointed, the film had the potential to be the perfect gift for lovers of 1950s science-fiction pulp, and at times it comes so close to realizing that dream, but just as often it feels like everyone involved felt as though they were superior to the source material. Then again, it is just that kind of odd film where its schizophrenic nature actually adds to its fascination and charm.

MARS ATTACKS! is only loosely based on the bubble gum cards which inspired it (the original gum cards were simply called *Mars Attacks*: the film added the exclamation point to the title, which is how the two will be differentiated here). While both film and cards tell the tale of an invasion from Mars, and both share the same sense of design for the Martians and their silver flying saucers, that is essentially where the plot similarities end (though the film does also pay visual homage to some of the individual cards). In **MARS ATTACKS!**, an army of UFOs encircle the Earth, hovering patiently as the US President (Jack Nicholson) and his aides try to determine if the extraterrestrial visitors are peaceful or malignant. A first contact meeting, set up in the Nevada desert, quickly descends into

Mars Needs Women! One of the more restrained cards in the *MA* series

Despite the all-star human cast, it's the impish E.T. shit-disturbers of **MARS ATTACKS!** who are the *real* stars of the show

chaotic slaughter after a hippie releases a dove as a gesture of peace, sparking off a widespread invasion of Earth, the pesky little Martians leaving a trail of destruction in their wake before meeting their match in the form of Slim Whitman's yodeling 1952 version of "Indian Love Call", the notes of which cause the invaders' bulbous brains to explode in a mass of green goo—a far cry from the more predictable climax of the bubble gum card set, in which Earthmen retaliate by blasting-off for Mars and bombing the planet into oblivion (in true Cold War military fashion!).

Tim Burton constructs **MARS ATTACKS!** like a series of vignettes and set-pieces rather than as a straight narrative. Though the film remains fairly cohesive, tonal shifts are all over the place. Some of the ensemble cast seem to be in on the joke (such as Pierce Brosnan's optimistic, pipe-smoking professor) while others, like Pam Grier, play it deadly serious. Apart from his role as the US President, Nicholson is also unwisely cast as a secondary character, an oily Las Vegas real estate scam artist living with a new age, recovering alcoholic wife (Annette Bening). Others in the over-crammed cast include Glenn Close as the First Lady, Natalie Portman as her disassociated daughter, Rod Steiger as a war-mongering army general who wants to nuke the Martian visitors on sight ("Annihilate! Kill! *Kill!! KILL!!!*"), Sarah Jessica Parker as a ditzy daytime TV host, Michael J. Fox as her more respected news reporter boyfriend, and Martin Short as a sleazy White House press secretary. There's also star footballer-turned-actor Jim Brown, veteran Sylvia Sidney, Christina Applegate, Joe-Don Baker, a young Jack Black and cameos from Danny DeVito, singer Tom Jones (as himself) and, perhaps most odd of all, respected film director Barbet Schroeder (**BAR-**

FLY [1987], **SINGLE WHITE FEMALE** [1992, both USA]) as the French President.

Despite its frustrating unevenness, there is still so much about **MARS ATTACKS!** to embrace and enjoy. The design of the film is mostly wonderful: a vibrant, colorful comic book come to pulsating life (something sorely missed in an age when so many genre films dwell on verisimilitude and grit). The Martians are an inspired creation. Short in stature but full of cheeky arrogance, they visually stay faithful to the original gum cards (the art on which was provided by Norman Saunders and Wally Wood), with the addition of some glittery green and purple capes to identify the senior Martians (the Supreme Commander seems to take a liking to 1960s back issues of *Playboy!*). They also speak in a quirky, high-pitched squawk—achieved by playing a duck's quack in reverse—and have some real personality to them, unlike so many other cinematic aliens. They have a sense of mischief to them that is genuinely endearing and charming.

While it would have been neat to have seen the Martians created via old-fashioned stop-motion animation (as originally planned before being ditched due to budgetary constraints), the CGI for the most part is effectively realized. That's not to say it is always photorealistic—at times far from it—but it certainly suits the film's gaudy, comic book color palette. Unfortunately, the movie doesn't feature any of the giant spiders or other creepy-crawlies which are shown chewing on folks in the gum cards, nor the infamous frost ray either, but there are some elements of the cards which made it into Jonathan Gem's screenplay: the burning cattle (which opens the film in a surreal fashion), the attack on Washington, the shrinking ray and the (very cool) giant Martian robot are all in there.

While some of the humor falls pretty flat (both in retrospect and at the time of its production), **MARS ATTACKS!** is peppered with a number of inventive and very funny visual and aural gags. Some of my favorites include the Martians being spooked by a tube of lipstick; the dodgy (manmade) Martian-to-English translator spitting out the words "Do not run! We are your *friends!*" as they run around zapping people into oblivion; the wicked experiments they perform on their human captives (seemingly for no other purpose than their own amusement); and the hilarious way in which the Martians deal with the threat of a nuclear missile. And how can one forget the stunning Lisa Marie as the Martian spy girl, her big bulbous brain hidden under a blonde beehive, chewing oxygen gum (*à la* Marine Boy) as she insinuates her way into the White House thanks to the Press Secretary's penchant for Washington hookers. She looks eerily beautiful, and the way she silently glides across the floor is ethereal and stunning. The whole sequence with her in it provides one of the real highlights of the film.

Released in December of 1996, **MARS ATTACKS!** failed to make much of an impact at the box-office, and was probably the first real sign of a chink in the Tim Burton armor. Unlike **ED WOOD**, the critics weren't very kind to **MARS ATTACKS!**, either. The film seemed to be a tough one to market (though the poster did have a great tagline: "*Nice Planet – We'll Take It!*"), and it didn't have the predictable tent-pole format which had helped make Roland Emmerich's **INDEPENDENCE DAY** such a huge hit earlier in the year. The irony of Burton helming a bomb straight after making a film about Ed Wood was not lost on some people. Though in the big alien invasion war of 1996, I have to say that **MARS ATTACKS!** certainly wins out in terms of design and creativity, and overall fun too.

Before heading into **MARS ATTACKS!**, Burton's original plan was to adapt Topps' 1988 gum card series *Dinosaurs Attack!* (see p.81), but he abandoned that idea, as Spielberg's **JURASSIC PARK** (1993, USA) was already in production and quickly gaining hype. Not wishing to compete, or appear to be riding on the coattails of the upcoming dinosaur juggernaut, Burton turned his attention to *Mars Attacks*, another notorious Topps card set, one that he remembered fondly from his own youth. Though he ditched the *Dinosaurs Attack!* idea, the tone and spirit of that card set certainly lives on in the **MARS ATTACKS!** film. Though a few of the original *Mars Attacks* cards displayed a hint of ghoulish humor, the set was pretty much a straightforward, if highly graphic, sci-fi invasion story which paid homage to the genre B-movies and comic books of a decade earlier. By comparison, Burton's film is filled with the kind of gags and satire which made up a huge part of the charm of the *Dinosaurs Attack!* cards. So it's interesting to look upon **MARS ATTACKS!** as a potential peek at the style and tone which a Burton-helmed *Dinosaurs Attack!* movie might have had (perhaps it was in tribute that the exclamation mark was added to the film's title?).

At the time of its release, **MARS ATTACKS!** was heavily merchandised, spawning a nice line of action figures by Trendmasters (my favorite being the Martian Spy Girl). The same company also produced a larger talking Martian figure, and a very cool silver Martian Saucer, that made some authentically retro space sounds and had firing missiles and an opening cockpit with tiny Martian pilot. Naturally, Topps reissued the original card set, as well as issuing a brand new set (in a longer "widescreen" format) featuring photographs from the movie. A Topps comic book was also published, along with several *Mars Attacks!* paperback novels and more. The disappointing box-office of the movie, however, saw much of the merchandise quickly discontinued and taken off the shelves.

Though the movie may have been a commercial failure, the *Mars Attacks* phenomena thankfully lives on, with recent years seeing the release of comic books, model kits, action figures, masks, bobble-head toys, reissues of the original card set, and much more. Though a film sequel may seem like a stretch, a *Mars Attacks* animated film, recreating the story of the original cards, would certainly be a welcome possibility...and one I hope to someday see.

NEXT ISSUE IN THE CONTINUING ADVENTURES OF THE HOUSE OF RAMSAY:

F.U. RAMSAY presents

आखरी चीख

RAMSAY MOVIES

AAKHRI CHEEKH

PRODUCED BY
RESHMA RAMSAY

MUSIC
BAPPI LAHIRI

LYRICS
**ANJAAN
ANWAR SAGAR**

COLOR BY ADLAB

WRITTEN & DIRECTED BY **KIRAN RAMSAY**

A CRAZY KILLER RETURNS FROM THE DEAD TO STALK THOSE WHO PUT HIM IN THE ELECTRIC CHAIR! CRAZY MONSTER ACTION FROM KIRAN "SHAITANI ILAAKA" RAMSAY!

THE HOUSE OF RAMSAY PART EIGHT

by Tim Paxton

The corpse-ghost of Christina rises from her grave thirsting for vengeance

GHUTAN

Reviewed by Tim Paxton

India, 2007. D: Shyam Ramsay

By the time **GHUTAN** was made, the Ramsay era of horror film dominance had come to an end. That family of Bollywood filmmakers had a wild fifteen years of ups and downs full of great and not-so-great monster movies. The most popular (and thus successful) where produced between 1978-91, when films like **DARWAZA** (1978), **PURANA MANDIR** (1984), **VEERANA** (1988), and **BANDH DARWAZA** (1990)[1] were box-office hits. But their popularity waned in the early 1990s and receipts dried up. This may have been due to a bored audience seeking other less-dated thrills in the films of their rivals. Tulsi Ramsay, who codirected many of their hits with his brother Shyam, sees it differently. In a recent interview he remarked, "People overdid it. After us, several people started to make bad horror films and every channel picked up the horror show idea. The audiences got sick of it."[2] I'm sure he was referring to the cheapjack productions that flooded the market, but not all of them were "bad horror films". Ram Gopal Varma's **RAAT** (1992) was one of the few horror films of the early 1990s that was a box office hit, and its altogether different approach was the herald of things to come.

An ad from the Indian pressbook for **GHUTAN** which features the "patented" Ramsay Sex & Horror" approach to filmmaking

---

[1] **PURANA MANDIR** and **BANDH DARWAZA** were both reviewed in past issues of *Monster!*: respectively, issues #4 (p.9) and #3 (p.49)

[2] *http://www.dnaindia.com/entertainment/report-the-requiem-for-ramsays-horror-1842613*

91

Poster for **BACHAO**, a 2010 Ramsay comedy-horror film which may eventually be released on DVD in mid-2015

The Ramsays tried their hand at TV production around the time that their last marketable film, a **NIGHTMARE ON ELM STREET** rip-off called **MAHAKAAL** (1993 [see *Monster!* #2, p.37]), saw less-than-profitable returns. Shyam Ramsay, his daughter Saasha and his brother Tulsi did manage a hot TV series that ran for a few years on Zee TV during 1993-98, and it was called "The Zee Horror Show." They also had to contend with the flood of cheap horror films from the likes of Kanti Shah, Jeetsu, and others whose titles were very close if not the same as classic Ramsay films.[3] The TV series did rather well, and the Ramsay Brothers attempted another launch into the theatres with Deepak's ghost film **AATMA** (2006 [see *M!* #9, p.61]) and then again in 2007 with Shyam's **GHUTAN**, the present film under review. While not horrible films, these two latter-day productions lacked what I had come to expected from the Ramsays: a good old-fashioned hoary monster. But ghosts were the rage then as they are now, so the hulking horrors were jettisoned for the like of *aatmas*, *bhoots*, or *mohonis*.

GHUTAN, like **AATMA**, came out post during the new boom in Indian horror films. This could be called the post-**BHOOT** era. **BHOOT**, which was released in 2003 to both critical and financial success (it was a blockbuster by Indian film stan-dards) is an extremely influential ghost film by Ram Gopal Varma…and yet another nail in the Ramsay Brothers International's coffin. Beginning in1998 and through 2007 when **GHUTAN** was made, the Ramsays had to deal with the new brand of "Bolly-wood"[4] horror film which included **RAAZ** (2002, D: Vikram Bhatt), **HAWA** (2003, D: Guddu Dhanoa), **SAAYA** (2003, D: Anurag Basu), **KRISHNA COTTAGE** (2004, D: Santram Varma), **FEAR** (2007, D: Vikram Bhatt), **DARLING** (2007, D: Ram Gopal Varma), **SIVI** (2007, D: K. R. Senthil Nathan), and **GAURI: THE UNBORN** (2007, D: Akku Akbar), to name only a few. What these films brought to the screen was new, slick, sexy, and very different from anything that the Ramsays had ever produced. There was no way they could compete. Deepak's **AATMA** tried to be like its contemporaries, but the result was rather like a monkey dancing in front of a mirror without completely understanding what it is mimicking.

The Ramsays had to come up with something to compete with this the new brand of ghostly cinema. Their past hits were monster movies, and when they did dabble in hauntings, the results were less than stellar (e.g., 1981's **HOTEL** [see *Monster!* #9, p.59]). Their relatively recent productions **AATMA** and **GHUTAN** were very brutal ghost films, and in a way that made them unique throwbacks, but they still lacked a certain *je ne sais quoi* of bygone flicks. In my opinion, the family dealt with physical, flesh and blood monsters better than with the more ethereal brand of critters; it's that simple. And the more goonish monsters the better, please! In a rather crude attempt to stay relevant, Shyam made a "sexy" vampire film in 2014—namely **NEIGHBOURS: THEY ARE VAMPIRES** (see *M!* #12, p.35)—and the result was less than classic. Granted he wasn't the only person to try a different approach to their films, as director Vikram Bhatt also attempted to buck the trend when he made **CREATURE 3D** (2014 [see *M!* #10.,p.11]); Bhatt's first full-on monster movie, which featured a huge scaly demon snacking on a hotel full of guests. Bhatt had been very successful in Bollywood with his previous ghost films, but **CREATURE 3D** failed miserably.

So, on with **GHUTAN**:

The film opens as car winds its way through the grounds of a local Christian cemetery. It stops and out climb a man and his male companion. They open the back door of the car and lug out an empty coffin along with the body of a battered and bloodied woman. At first we assume she must be dead, considering

---

[3] **SAAMRI** (2000, D: K.L. Sheiki), **DAAK BANGLA** (2000, D: R. Mittal), **DAHSHAT** (2000, D: Sailesh Konchady), **TAHKHANA** (2001, D: Kishan Shah)

[4] Just to make this clear, Bollywood should not be used to describe all movies made in India. Bollywood refers to Hindi-language productions, and primarily those made in and around Mumbai (once known as Bombay). Other states in India have their own play on Hollywood depending on their language.

the extent of her wounds and the two men's obvious intention of burying her in the graveyard. However, she *isn't*, and her eyes suddenly pop open. When she realizes she is about to be buried alive, she begs for her life. She is manhandled into the coffin and the lid is nailed shut. She screams and threatens, but the coffin is pushed into an open grave and the two men hurriedly pile dirt upon it. Her pleas and curses become increasing more frantic and faint as the hole is filled and a large stone cross is dumped atop the fresh mound of dirt. The two scoundrels drive off, and she is left alone to suffocate in an unmarked grave...

So goes the fairly straightforward beginning to the last good horror film from the Ramsays. After **GHUTAN** there was the comedy horror **BACHAO – INSIDE BHOOT HAI...** (2010, D: Shyam Ramsay), a film I would love to review if I could find a copy (it has never, to my knowledge, been released on VCD, DVD, or streaming on any video service). Last issue I reviewed **NEIGHBOURS: THEY ARE VAMPIRES**, which was Shyam's very weak return to horror; yet another rip-off of Tom Holland's **FRIGHT NIGHT** (1985, USA). It, like **AATMA**, **GHUTAN**, and **BACHAO** bombed at the box office. Of the three most recent Ramsay films that I have seen, **GHUTAN** was the closest one to have replicated the feel of their classics. What follows next in the present film after the opening sequence described above is highly typical of the *mohoni* ghost subgenre, and isn't at all innovative. This is not to say that the film sucked. The colorful cinematography aside, **GHUTAN** is a serviceable enough horror film which delivers a few effective scenes without *too* many instances of banal comedy and only one truly horrible musical interlude along the way.

As it turns out, a goodly chunk of the film unfolds in flashback, depicting events just prior to the delivery of the woman to her lonely death in the graveyard. Ravi Kapoor (Aryan Vaid) is a business man who is squandering the company's fortunes on bad investments and women. His wife, Catherine (Heena Tasleem), is a boozy harpy who only wants her husband to love her. She sits at her grand piano in their spacious home playing melodramatic tunes and guzzling bottles of wine. Ravi ignores her advances, interested in making time with Priya (Pooja Bharti), his new secretary. Catherine suspects that her husband is cheating on her, and confronts Ravi. They have a very vocal argument that turns physical and Ravi strikes his wife, sending her flying off a balcony inside their home and crashing through a plate glass dinner table. Ravi freaks when he is unable to revive Catherine and gets his best friend Jaggi to help him dispose of the body. This is all seen by the housemaid Nancy, who is threatened into silence by the brutish Ravi. The two men then stow Catherine's body in their car, pick up an empty coffin and head

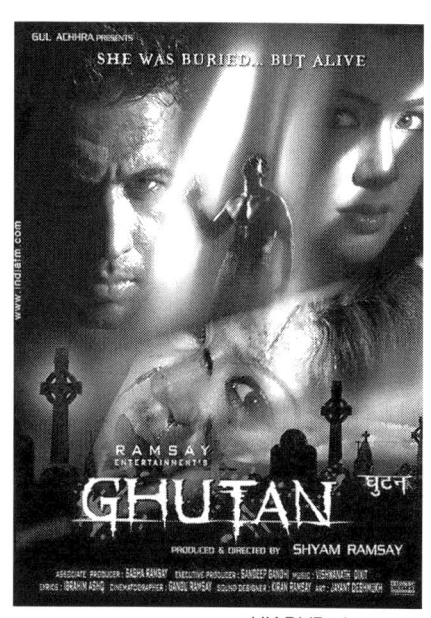

UK DVD sleeve art

out to the nearby cemetery.

The film's one truly effective sequence shortly follows, when Catherine manages to break through the coffin lid and dig herself out of the ground. She stumbles away from the graveyard and makes her way to the nearby Catholic church, where she seeks out her family priest, Father James. She stands before the priest and blurts out everything that has happened to her. He looks at Catherine only to turn away from her, and a troubled sadness fills his eyes as he says that he can't help her because she is... *already dead!* Catherine reaches out to hold onto Father James' hand, only to have it pass clear through his. Horrified that her husband has killed her, she is determined to have her revenge by reentering her body and hunting down Ravi, her "dearly beloved". Against the pleas of Father James, Catherine's ghost returns to her grave and reenters her body... whereupon she becomes an evil spirit: a *mohoni*, the classic vengeful female ghost of Indian folklore.

GHUTAN took an hour to get to this point, and when it finally takes off, it does so when Catherine haunts her husband's home and terrorizes his new girlfriend Priya. Her haunting and threatening gets so bad that Priya goes to a New Age[5] "professor" whose spe-

---

[5] Ah, yes, in a way the New Age movement comes full circle in **GHUTAN**. The popular image of the New Age practitioner seen in the film (crystals, channeling spirits and all) is a more-or-less direct descendant of two Russian 19th Century antecedents, Helena Blavatsky and G.I. Gurdjieff, who, along with the Indian Swami Vivekananda, incorporated Hindu mysticism into their esoteric philosophy, which eventually mutated into the annoying form of spiritualism we know it as today.

cialty is dealing with rambunctious spirits. He consults his crystals and manages to channel the ghost, who then spills the beans even though Priya doesn't want to believe that her new boyfriend is a murderer. Catherine hunts down Jaggi and breaks his neck, subsequently confronts Father James and boils his brains, then possesses Nancy, who attacks her employer, but Ravi is able to kill her when she attacks him. Ravi flees for his life, whereupon he is chased into the very same graveyard where he prematurely entombed Catherine. There Ravi battles his former wife in hand-to-hand combat. She screeches and tears at his clothes, leaving him bare-chested and without a shirt (providing some beefcake for the audience, as actor Aryan Vaid was also a well-known male model). Ravi fights back, flexing his muscles as he swings a huge marble grave-marker like baseball bat. He manages to clock Catherine a few times as the she-ghost flies around him. Eventually, as fate would have it, the screeching spirit manages to knock her husband into her open grave, where both are covered in dirt and buried alive (well, in his case, if not hers, she being dead already).

So, did I like the film? Surprisingly, I did. I had very low expectations when I finally got around to watching **GHUTAN**, as I steeled myself for another round of CG-filled cheap Bollywood effects. Instead what I saw was mostly practical effects, which was odd considering that even in 2007 CG was used extensively in similarly-themed (and cheaper) productions. The aforementioned **NEIGHBOURS**, on the other hand, had most of its potential horror elements cheesed-up by ridiculously bad postproduction CG, thanks to the low-budget effects company FX Factory (and, from the looks of the film's trailer, so does the above-cited **BACHAO – INSIDE BHOOT HAI...**, too). Most of **GHUTAN**'s pretty cinematography and vibrancy comes thanks to Gangu Ramsay, whose work for this film reminds me of S. Pappu's classic Bavaeqsue color schemes utilized on many of the classics, including two of my favorites: **DAK BANGLA** and **SHAITANI ILAAKA** (both 1990 [see *M!* #2, p.39 and #8, p.5, respectively]); as well as his past work on **TAHKHANA** (1986 [see *M!* #3, p.53]) and **BANDH DARWAZA** (1990 [*M!* #3, p.49]). Gangu's work here allows the film to bask in an unreal vintage '80s atmosphere which only enhances the liberal amounts of wirework, fog machines, and the overuse of lighting and thunder effects (typically only used when the *mohini* is skulking on the set).

As for the monster in **GHUTAN**, Catherine is your basic *mohini*, and actress Hina Tasleem does a splendid job chewing up the scenery (then again, all involved crank-up the overacting to the nth degree!). She is dressed in her grave clothes, as per custom for such supernatural creatures, and floats in the air, screams, and curses, alternately existing on both the corporeal and non-corporeal planes.

Her scarred face is nothing new in Indian horror, either. That similar pattern of slashes can be seen in earlier Malayalam and Tamil horror films like **PATHIMOONAM NUMBER VEEDU** (1990, D: A.G. Baby), for example.[6] Many Indian films from the 1970s, '80s and '90s borrowed their "look" from Dick Smith's world-famous makeup for Linda Blair as the possessed Regan in William Friedkin's mega-hit **THE EXORCIST** (1973, USA). Funny how that one film is *still* influential on Indian horror movies to this day, even in a predominantly non-Christian culture. Besides the levitating bed, projectile vomit, and bad attitude of the possessed, each of the haunted women have pretty much the exact same scarification makeup, which can also be seen in **1920** (2008, D: Vikram Bhatt), **CHEMISTRY** (2009, D: Viji Thampi), **AA INTLO** (2009, D: Chinna), and others.

However, while **GHUTAN** was full of the same motifs that other directors utilized in their hits, the film nonetheless still flopped. And the total boxoffice receipts are an all-important element in Indian cinema—much more so it seems than in the USA. Here in the States, if a film tanks it can still be a critical darling and make its money back in DVD sales (Pete Travis' unbelievably good **DREDD** [2012, UK/USA/India/South Africa] is one example), but in India it is deemed unworthy and may never be seen again. So, I throw it out to you, Shyam, if you ever want to get your films once again recognized for being what they once were, you have three choices: One, stop announcing that "Ramsay Horror is Back!" and sucking on that heady pipedream of your past glories—for instance, the Ramsays are proposing a remake of/sequel to one of their best films, **VEERANA**; which is gonna be tough, because that film's stunning actress Jasmine has all but vanished off the face of the Earth—and take a look around at what is in the theatres *now*. Check out the competition. Two, *please stop ripping-off* Hollywood! You and other filmmakers have an entire subcontinent of lore and spookiness to ransack for your horror films (hell, I'll even write you a treatment). You've done it in the past, you can do it again.

Oh, and, three, for the gods' sake, stop utilizing cheap CG. Please. It's horrible!

Endnote: Just when you think I may be running out of monster films from the Ramsays, I have just discovered that there are some composite movies made from episodes of *The Zee Horror Show* on YouTube, and some of them even have English subtitles and honest-to-god monsters. I couldn't let you guys off the hook that easy!

---

6 Reviewed in *Weng's Chop* #4.5, p.117

MONStER! #13 MOVIE CHECKLISt
MONSTER! Public Service posting: Title availability of films reviewed or mentioned in this issue of MONSTER!
Information dug up and presented by Steve Fenton and Tim Paxton.

<u>The Fine Print</u>: Unless otherwise noted, all Blu-rays and DVDs listed in this section are in the NTSC Region A/Region 1 format and widescreen, as well as coming complete with English dialogue (i.e., were either originally shot in that language, or else dubbed/subbed into it). If there are any deviations from the norm, such as full-frame format, discs from different regions or foreign-language dialogue (etc.), it shall be duly noted under the headings of the individual entries below.

ALIEN APOCALYPSE (p.51) – Put out on domestic DVD in 2005 (at 1.77:1 widescreen) by Anchor Bay Entertainment. Extras include audio commentary by star Bruce Campbell and writer-director Josh Becker, plus a behind-the-scenes featurette. AB reissued it in the same disc format with different packaging in 2007. Said packaging, depicting Campbell toting a big smoking gun in one hand and a crossbow in the other, blatantly—if by no means unexpectedly—evoked his Ash character from Raimi's *Evil Dead* series.

ALIEN HUNTER (p.50) – British DVD ad-line: "*There IS Something Out There!*" Released on domestic DVD by Columbia/Tristar Video in 2003. The same company also issued it in the same format in a number of other foreign countries, evidently all of those non-domestic versions also coming complete with an original English-language dialogue option in addition to either an optional audio track or subs in the vernacular of whatever outside market it was released into. So those with all-region DVD players should be able to pick themselves up a copy from just about anywhere and chances are it'll come with English (assuming you need it, that is!).

BRAIN 17 (p.55) – Originally (*circa* the late '80s) put out on domestic N. American VHS/Beta videocassette by the kidvid label Family Home Entertainment (FHE). A passably watchable rip of said English-dubbed tape version is up for view on YouTube (@ *https://www.youtube.com/watch?v=IJkG-d_u_95A*). We highly doubt there has been any legit digital disc release of this (?), but DVD-R copies of FHE's erstwhile version may well be being flogged somewhere online via grey market sources. For all we know, the entire original series may have been released on Japanese disc. At the link titled (備り) 大鐵人17號_26 (永別了!18號) there is at least one episode, #26, uploaded to YouTube (@ the URL addy *https://www.youtube.com/watch?v=sgaI1BEMBr0*), but it only comes in its original Japanese, with Chinese subtitles and no English. Numerous related clips and other ephemera—including at least one vintage toy commercial—can also be found at YT. In order to access the links, simply visit the show's Wikipedia page (@ *http://en.wikipedia.org/wiki/Daitetsujin_17*), copy over the original title's *kanji* characters, then paste them into the search at YT. Plenty of links will pop up!

CREATURES FROM THE ABYSS (p.48) – Celebrated golden age SF author Murray Leinster wrote a similarly-titled novel (ad-line: "*From the ocean depths terror stalked mankind!*") called *Creatures of the Abyss* (a.k.a. *The Listeners*, Berkley Books, 1961), and top '70s fantasy novel cover illustrator Boris Vallejo painted a sea monster-meets-female-scuba-diver illustration entitled "Creatures from the Abyss" (1971); but it rather goes without saying that there is no connection between either of those and the present title! In 2001, the film was issued on domestic DVD by Shriek Show in a "Widescream [*sic!*] Edition" (at a 1.85:1 aspect ratio). As of this writing, a number of copies of Shriek Show's edition were up for grabs dirt-cheap on both Amazon and eBay. SS also issued it as part of their 3-film, 3-disc "Mutant Monsters Triple Feature" set, a rather mismatched hodgepodge of only (very) loosely-connected monster titles also including John "Bud" Cardos' and Tobe Hooper's

95

Hell is hungry.

"A gut-flinging monster mash." - Dread Central

"Destined for midnight movie immortality." - Bloody Disgusting

THE DEMON'S ROOK

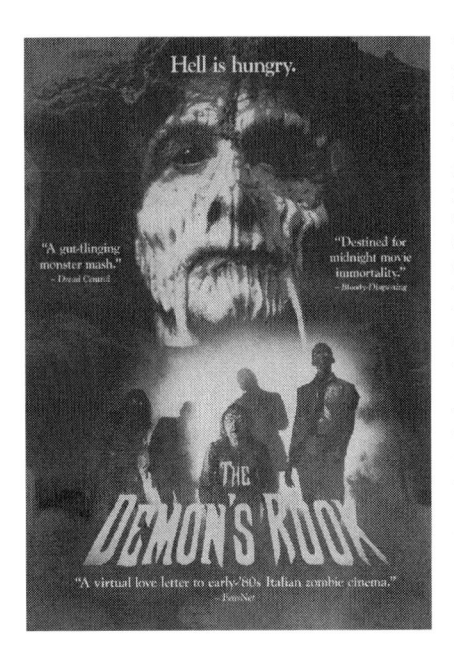

"A virtual love letter to early-'80s Italian zombie cinema." - FanNet

killer E.T. thriller **THE DARK** (1979, USA) along with Jackie Kong's endearingly earnest if humble **ALIEN**-imitative toxic mutant SF/horror cheapie **THE BEING** (1983, USA) which is a lot more fun than its measly "3.4" rating at the IMDb might lead you to expect.

CURSE OF EVIL (p.53) – A grey market, widescreen, so-called "Remastered Version" DVD-R— loudly if unofficially bearing the Shaw Bros. logo—is available for $10 from Far East Flix (@ http://www.fareastflix.com/shaw-brothers/curse-of-evil/). Earlier in the 21st Century, it was presumably (?) numbered among the scads and scads of Shaw titles officially released onto Hong Kong DVD by them, and would have come with an English subs option and multiple other language options like the rest did.

THE DEMON'S ROOK (p.57) – Available on DVD from Tribeca Films. For a mere $3.99 rental fee, it is also viewable VOD on Vudu, Amazon, iTunes or YouTube (a number of official HD trailers and behind-the-scenes mini-docs for the film can also be viewed at that latter site). For those interested, same director James Sizemore's creepy, supernatural-steeped horror short subject *Goat Witch* (2014, USA)—a mere (unlucky?) 13 minutes long—is legitimately available to view gratis on Vimeo (@ http://vimeo.com/100747052), as is also a way-cool, well-edited 3-minute making-of featurette, set to music sans any voiceover, about said short (@ http://vimeo.com/100338270). Those who gravitate towards movies featuring diabolical demonstrosities, horny head-ripping wicked witch bitches from hell, monk-cassocked zombies *à la*

The Blind Dead, pagan/wiccan/diabolist occultism, extreme splatter and (*bonus!*) full-frontal female nudity—mostly from the director's lithe wife, Ashleigh Jo Sizemore—and even some bestiality-tinged lesbo lovemaking will definitely want to give *GW* a look-see… and, at such a brief duration, you won't have to waste too much of your valuable time to do so. A major influence on certain key aspects of the film was obviously Dario Argento's and Lamberto Bava's batshit-crazy demonic contagion shocker **DEMONS** (*Dèmoni*, 1985, Italy), but this well-stuffed, excellently put together short crams in all sorts of other (chiefly '80sesque) influences too, and it really does generate a dense and intoxicatingly/hypnotically eldritch atmosphere, whose roughly closest equivalent in dark tone that we can think of is still photographer-turned-filmmaker Avery Crounse's unsettling yet at the same time often lyrical period backwoods horror tale **EYES OF FIRE** (1983, USA); and make no mistake, for all its dark ambience, there is some real visual poetry going on in *GW*. The short is sumptuously shot by DP Tim Reis of **THE DEMON'S ROOK**, and, as in that feature-length film, *Goat Witch*'s wondrously fleshy (rather than phonily rubbery),100% practical special makeup FX—especially those for the horned, hooved humanoid billygoat demon Yomowen, played by Josh Adam Gould—are truly exemplary, beating out most synthetic CG critters hands-down, no contest. We can only hope that such TLC-driven productions as this are the wave of the future!

GHUTAN (p.91) – Anglo ad-lines: *"She Was Buried… But Alive. Her Body Gave Way… Her Soul Didn't. She Still Breathes In Her Coffin"*. Available on All-Region DVD from Madhu Entertainment, with English subtitles. As of this writing, copies were on offer at Amazon for a penny short of ten bucks. On eBay I saw a copy (in different packaging) with a price-tag of a mere $2.49; there was also a pressbook for the film up for auction at the same site (with a starting bid of $10.20). For just two quid (i.e., £2.00), this A-R disc is also available from the British retail site Apollo DVD (@ the link http://www.apollodvd.co.uk/html/Product_display.asp?proID=2438&catID=166). It has also been released as part of a "3in1" triple-bill DVD or VCD also including Shyam Ramsay's **NEIGHBOURS: THEY ARE VAMPIRES** (2014, India [see *Monster!* #12]) and another recent Indian horror thriller, Sanjay Khandelwal's ghost story **ROOH** (2010). Check *Induna.com* for availability.

THE GIANT GILA MONSTER (p.62) – Formerly available on VHS tape from Sinister Cinema, Something Weird Video, Rhino Home Video and VCI Home Video (etc). As recently as 2004, it was released in the same tape format by both Diamond Entertainment Group and Reel Media International. For those who feel they need it,

Mystery Science Theater 3000's—ahem—"modified" version is available both on DVD and as an Amazon insta-vid in SD-only mode, for $2.99 to rent and $11.99 to buy. Interestingly, Jim Wynorski's made-for-TV partial remake/homage **GILA!** (2012, USA)—which includes a special guest cameo by the original '59 film's star, Don Sullivan—is also available at the same site for purchase/rental in either HD ($13.95/$3.95) or SD ($3.95/$2.95). For our money, better it than *MS3TK*'s piss-take on the founding film... but rather than spew any more bile about it, we'll leave it at that (talk about exercise tactful restraint!). In 2014, **GILA!** was also made available on domestic DVD by Polyscope Media Group, presented at its original small screen aspect ratio of 1.33:1 (full-frame). As for the present film, it has been put out on domestic DVD by a number of labels, most recently (in 2014) by Mutant Sorority Pictures as an All-Region release. Prior to that, it was variously sold on disc—with presumably wildly varying levels of picture quality, so shop wisely!—by such other American companies as Elite Entertainment, K-Tel Video, Madacy Entertainment, Alpha Video Distributors, Englewood Entertainment, Gotham Distribution, Image Entertainment, Navarre Entertainment, EastWest Entertainment and Genius Entertainment. Of all those, our guess would be that either Image's or Elite's would look the nicest (?). It was also included as part of Gaiam Americas' 2012 collection "12 Drive-In Theatre Cult Classics". There are assorted different rips of variable picture quality uploaded to YouTube, including *MS3TK*'s version and even a heavily-abbreviated (22+-minute), colorized version which aired on Canadian TV *circa* the mid-'90s in a half-hour timeslot as part of a "cult cinema" series—produced by Toronto-based animation house Nelvana, of all people—entitled *The Attack of the Killer 'B' Movies* (which has nothing whatsoever to do with the 1995 "*MST3K*" homage" of the same title).

Hammer's DRACULA series (pp.24-37) – Simply because there are so many different releases of these films, due to limited space availability we are only listing some examples. Series entry #1: Under its North American theatrical release title of **HORROR OF DRACULA**, the film is available domestically on DVD from Warner Home Video. In 2013, under its original British title of simply **DRACULA** (p.25), it was issued in a deluxe, extras-crammed 3-disc edition by Lionsgate UK in the PAL Region B Blu-ray format. #2: **DRACULA – PRINCE OF DARKNESS** (p.27) was issued on DVD by Starz/Anchor Bay (including in a 2004 2-disc edition paired with #7 in the series). It was put out on Blu-ray in 2013 by Exclusive Media Group. #3: **DRACULA HAS RISEN FROM THE GRAVE** (p.29) was issued on DVD in 2004 by Warner. #4: **TASTE THE BLOOD OF DRACULA** (p.31) was made available on DVD by Warner Home Video in 2004. In 2005 it was released in a single disc double bill with **THE CURSE OF FRANKENSTEIN** (see next entry heading below). #5: **SCARS OF DRACULA** (p.32) was released on domestic Lionsgate DVD in 2012. #6: **DRACULA A.D. 1972** (p.34) was released on DVD by Warner in 2005. #7: **THE SATANIC RITES OF DRACULA** (p.35) was put out in 2003 as a fugly fullscreen version by Alpha Video (*buyer beware!*). A much nicer widescreen version was issued by Starz/Anchor Bay, and the film is currently available in several versions on Amazon as VOD streaming Instant Videos (including a "Synergy Archives Series" version under its alternate US theatrical release title of **COUNT DRACULA AND HIS VAMPIRE BRIDE**). There are many sub-par versions of this evidently now PD (?) title floating around, so be selective! The following "unofficial" #8 entry, **THE LEGEND OF THE 7 GOLDEN VAMPIRES** (p.36), is the only film in the series not to star Lee as Dracula. Back in 1999, Anchor Bay released the film in a single disc edition which also included an alternate cut of the film entitled **THE SEVEN BROTHERS MEET DRACULA**. More recently (2013) **LEGEND** became made available in a 2-disc DVD set by Millennium, triple-billed with the #2 Hammer Drac series film (see above) and the #4 film in the studio's *Frankenstein* series (see next entry heading below). In 2004, WB issued Drac films #1, #3 and #4 as part of their six-pack "Horror Classics Collection". In 2010, Warners repackaged the 1st, 3rd, 4th and 6th series entries in a 2-disc set simply entitled "Draculas" as part of its budget "4 Film Favorites" line, all in their proper widescreen presentations. The same year, Turner Classic Movies (TCM) issued the 1st and 3rd films in a 2-disc set which also included the 1st and 5th films in Hammer's *Frankenstein* series (see next entry heading below). In 2013, Millennium released the 2nd Drac film in a 2-disc DVD set along with the only-loosely-connected 8th series entry and the 4th film in the studio's *Frankenstein* series (see next entry heading below). **THE BRIDES OF DRACULA**—which, despite its title, doesn't really count (pun intended) as part of the series proper, because the vampire aristocrat in the film (David Peel) is actually named Baron Meinster, not Drac—was released onto domestic DVD in 2005 by Universal Studios Home Entertainment as part of their must-have 2-disc, 8-film set "The Hammer Horror Series Franchise Collection". All of the titles listed in this entry were variously released in the VHS/Beta cassette and/or laserdisc formats back in the '80s and '90s.

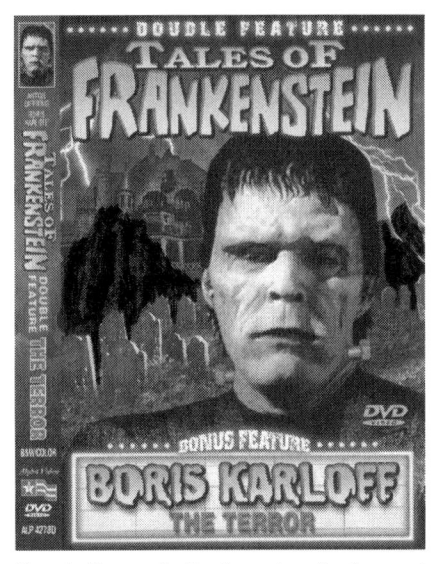

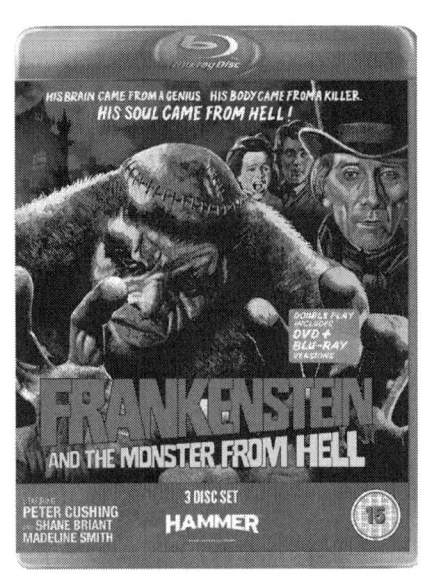

Hammer's FRANKENSTEIN series (pp.8-23) – Among Hammer's earliest forays into the exploits of the Mary Shelley-based mad doctor/monster characters was *Tales of Frankenstein* (1958, UK/USA), the unsold 28m. pilot—officially titled "The Face in the Tombstone Mirror"—for a proposed but never realized 13-episode teleseries; but it was in the developmental stage for some time and the ABC network was even considering picking it up before things fell apart, although certain themes from early drafts of potential scripts for the unrealized program later found their way into some of Hammer's cinematic series outings. A coproduction between Hammer and Columbia Pictures TV budgeted at around $80,000 and shot in Hollywood rather than over at Hammer's usual haunts, England's Bray Studios, it was produced, co-written and directed by Curt Siodmak, veteran of many a 1940s Universal Monsters classic (including **THE WOLF MAN** [1941]) who had written a pair of Unipix's own *Frankenstein* franchise (**FRANKENSTEIN MEETS THE WOLF MAN** [1943] and **HOUSE OF FRANKENSTEIN** [1944]), thus providing a direct link between the two studios most universally associated with horror movies. Strangely enough, while a Columbia coproduction, *ToF*'s intro montage utilizes snippets of stock footage from some of Universal's horror efforts of the '30s and '40s (even including a brief shot of Lugosi's vampire "brides" from Tod Browning's 1931 **DRACULA**!). In an interesting bit of casting—which might seem a bit of a no-brainer (pun intended) considering the actor's Germanic roots and strong *achzent*—Anton Diffring ("Your brain came from the skull of a murderer!") is here cast, much in the Cushing mold, if a more aquiline Aryan version, as the driven, morally barren Baron, and the following year Diffring (1918-1989) would memorably play the title role in Hammer's **THE MAN WHO COULD CHEAT DEATH** (1959, UK). Here appearing as "The Monster" with the defective brain is XL (6' 6") actor Don Megowan ([1922-1981] player of the surgically altered, air-breathing gillman in John Sherwood's final *Creature* trilogy outing **THE CREATURE WALKS AMONG US** and the human hero of Fred F. Sears' Atomic Age lycanthropy tale **THE WEREWOLF** [both 1956, USA]), who herein sports a makeup design clearly inspired by the classic Jack P. Pierce/Karloff creation, and at times Megowan's even looks rather like Glenn Strange's version of the manmade monster. And not only that, but the FX for the electrical gizmos in the lab strongly evoke Kenneth Strickfaden's iconic work. Well-acted and -produced and atmospherically shot in moody monochrome, the episode provides a promising foretaste of what might have been but which unfortunately was ultimately not to be; although we can at least be thankful that this pilot has stuck around for posterity rather than simply vanishing without a trace, as so many unsold pilots are prone to do. It was released on VHS in the '90s by Sinister Cinema, and was put out on domestic DVD in the '00s by various companies, including Image Entertainment, Alpha Video and All-Day Entertainment. (For more backstory on the pilot, visit Frankensteinia: The Frankenstein Blog @ the page *http://frankensteinia.blogspot.ca/2008/03/tales-of-frankenstein.html*). To conserve space, we're gonna keep these following vid listings for the rest of Hammer's Frankie series concise:- #1: **THE CURSE OF FRANKENSTEIN** ([p.11] Warner Home Video DVD [2002] and Double Play PAL Region B/2 Blu-ray/DVD combo). #2: **THE REVENGE OF FRANKENSTEIN** ([p.15] Sony Pictures Home Entertainment DVD [2002]). #3: **THE EVIL OF FRANKENSTEIN** ([pp.3 & 17] Universal Studios DVD [2005] as part of the 2-disc, 8-film "The Hammer Horror Series Franchise Collection"; and in a Double Play PAL Region B/2 Blu-ray/DVD combo [2013]). #4: **FRANKENSTEIN CREATED WOMAN** ([p.18] Starz/Anchor Bay DVD [2004] and Millennium/Hammer Blu-ray [2014]). #5: **FRANKENSTEIN MUST BE DESTROYED** ([p.20] Warner Home Video DVD [2004]). #6: **THE HORROR OF FRANKENSTEIN** ([p.21] Starz/Anchor Bay DVD [2001]). #7: **FRANKENSTEIN AND THE MONSTER FROM HELL** ([p.22] Paramount DVD [2003] and Icon Home Entertainment Region A/1 Blu-ray/DVD combo [2014]). Back in 2004, WB issued films #1 and #5 as part of their six-pack "Horror Classics Collection". In 2010, TCM issued the 1st and 5th films in a 2-disc set which also included the 1st and 3rd films in Hammer's *Dracula* series (see previous entry heading above). Most if not all of the series are streamable VOD online at various venues, Amazon included. There are virtually innumerable options open to you, and no shortage of copies available! For completist collectors of a more "retro" bent, all of the titles listed in this entry were variously released in the VHS/Beta cassette and/or laserdisc formats back in the '80s and '90s.

Universal's **FRANKENSTEIN** series (pp.3-7) – **FRANKENSTEIN, THE BRIDE OF FRANKENSTEIN, THE SON OF FRANKENSTEIN, THE GHOST OF FRANKENSTEIN, FRANKENSTEIN MEETS THE WOLF MAN, HOUSE OF FRANKENSTEIN, HOUSE OF DRACULA** and **ABBOTT AND COSTELLO MEET FRANKENSTEIN** are all available domestically on Blu-ray and/or DVD from Universal Studios Home Entertainment, plus are also viewable VOD via any number of online streaming sources.

I AM LEGEND (p.64) – Released on Blu-ray and DVD by Warner Home Video. Rentable or buyable as an Amazon Instant Video in either the HD ($3.99 to rent, $12.99 to buy) or SD ($2.99 or $9.99) qual- ity formats. For those same HD prices, a version of the film with an alternate ending is also available as a High Definition-only insta-vid at the same site. In 2012, the film was double-billed on DVD along with The Hughes Brothers' post-apocalyptic action adventure **THE BOOK OF ELI** (2010, USA), starring Denzel Washington; according to Amazon—whose listed specs aren't always reliable—the films are presented at a 1.33:1 (cropped, full-frame) aspect ratio... but your guess is as good as ours. Considering that both films were originally released in full 2.35:1 widescreen, that means some heavy cropping went down! Likewise allegedly (?) at a mere 1.33:1, in 2014 Warners also released **IAL** as part of a "4 Film Favorites" package deal under the group heading "Post-Apocalypse Collection"; a quartet of discs including the previous big screen adaptation of Richard Matheson's *I Am Legend* (**THE OMEGA MAN** [see separate entry below]), along with the Director's Cut of Alex Proyas' **DARK CITY** (1998, USA/Australia) and Michael Anderson's **LOGAN'S RUN** (1976, USA). More recently, **IAL** has also been paired-up on Warner Blu-ray with **THE OMEGA MAN** (wot, no **THE LAST MAN ON EARTH**?! ☺). There are trillions of copies of **IAL** in all its various digital disc incarnations for sale on Amazon, which also offers several different editions of Matheson's original source novel, as well as the 2008 graphic novel adaptation of same by Steve Niles and Elman Brown.

I AM OMEGA (p.69) – Issued on domestic Blu-ray (at 1.66:1) by Echo Bridge Home Entertainment in 2010. Also from Echo Bridge, it has been included as part of a sell-through 3-film, 1-disc set along with a pair of other cheapies c/o The Asylum, namely **AVH: ALIEN VS. HUNTER** (2007, USA) and the execrable **MONSTER** (2008, USA [see *Monster!* #11]).

THE LAST MAN ON EARTH (p.73) – Rentable or purchasable on Amazon as an SD-only Instant Video (for $2.99 to rent and $9.99 to buy); there is also a different insta-vid version of the same film there for rental/purchase, likewise solely in Standard Definition ($2.99/$5.00). Quite a few shoddy versions of this PD and frequently sloppily repackaged film have circulated on tape and disc over the years, so choose carefully! In 2008, Legend Films issued it on domestic widescreen DVD in a colorized version, but their disc thankfully also came with the original unaltered B&W version (which, at least according to an ad-blurb at Amazon, *"has been Beautifully Restored and Enhanced!"*). It was previously released on DVD by both Madacy Entertainment (2003) and Alpha Video (2004), who also offered widescreen prints. Most recently (2014), Shout! Factory compiled it as part of their 4-disc, 7-film DVD box set "The Vincent Price Collection II", collectively pack-

Italian limited edition 2-disc DVD set for
THE LAST MAN ON EARTH

aged with such other Price favorites as William Castle's **HOUSE ON HAUNTED HILL** (1958), Edward Bernds' **RETURN OF THE FLY** (1959, both USA), Jacques Tourneur's **THE COMEDY OF TERRORS**, Roger Corman's **THE RAVEN** (both 1963, USA), Corman's **TOMB OF LIGEIA** (1964, UK) and Robert Fuest's **DR. PHIBES RISES AGAIN** (1972, UK/USA). Back in 2002 in the same format (albeit full-frame at 1.33:1?), the Platinum Disc company released it in a single disc threesome along with the aforementioned **HOUSE ON HAUNTED HILL** and the 1959 Crane Wilbur remake of the hoary haunted house whodunit **THE BAT**, another VP starrer.

MARS ATTACKS! (p.87) – Originally put out on domestic DVD, laserdisc and VHS by Warner Home Video (in '97), it was much more recently (2012) also issued on Blu-ray by WB. It can currently be rented or purchased as an Amazon insta-vid, for $3.99 (HD) / $2.99 (SD) to rent or $12.99 (HD) / $9.99 (SD) to purchase. A heavily-illustrated 224-page hardcover book entitled *Mars Attacks* (published by Harry N. Abrams in 2012) is also up for grabs on Amazon, detailing the story/controversy behind the series of outrageously gruesome trading cards put out by the Topps company in 1962. As with the company's later *Dinosaurs Attack!* set (1988 [see p.81]), the *MA* cards have also been reprinted over the intervening years since they were first published.

THE OMEGA MAN (p.76) – Warner Home Video first put this out on DVD in the early years of the digital versatile disc medium (1999), at its proper 2.35:1 aspect ratio. In 2011 it was comped in WB's budget four-fer box set entitled "4 Film Favorites Charlton Heston Collection", bundled together with the Heston-directed outdoorsy treasure-hunting adventure **MOTHER LODE** (1982, USA), John Guillermin's action drama **SKYJACKED** (1972, USA) and—best of all—Richard Fleischer's dystopian futuristic SF "social drama" **SOYLENT GREEN** (1973, USA). **OMEGA** was also issued singly on Blu-ray by Warners in 2010, and was subsequently (2013) reissued by them both in a pair-up with the 2007 reboot **I AM LEGEND**, as well as in a Triple Feature which also repackaged two other '70s WB sci-fi cult favorites, **LOGAN'S RUN** and the aforementioned **SOYLENT GREEN**. (See also our separate **I AM LEGEND** entry above for other combo releases which include the present film.) As of this writing, there were numerous copies for sale on Amazon of Ron Grainer's soundtrack for the film, on an audio CD titled *The Omega Man 2.0 Unlimited*.

SNOWBEAST (p.39) – This title is available from any number of videos, including Alpha Video, BijouFlix Releasing, Image Entertainment, Legacy Entertainment, Mill Creek Entertainment, Retromedia Entertainment and Synergy Entertainment, etc. In 2001, it was included along with fuzzy pan-and-scan transfers of Bill Malone's great fun **ALIEN** rip-off **CREATURE** (a.k.a. **TITAN FIND**, 1985, USA) and Richard Ashe's **TRACK OF THE MOON BEAST** (1976, USA [see *Monster!* #1]) as the bottommost third of a triple-bill disc entitled "Classic Creature Movies", put out by the Canadian cheapo label American Home Treasures. There is a quite decent copy of the film on YouTube at the link titled "Snowbeast - Full Movie Creature Feature" (@ *https://www.youtube.com/watch?v=iELllKW-f7Q*).

SOULKEEPER (p.43) – Ad-line: *"Evil Hungers For Your Soul"*. Alternate ad-line: *"Evil Is Making A Comeback"*. Issued on DVD in 2001—boasting some of the crappiest cover art ever seen!—by ka-BOOM! Entertainment. It was also alternately released in only marginally less-crappy artwork by them that same year. Special features included two brief behind-the-scenes featurettes, plus an even briefer selection of stills. A Director's Cut DVD edition of the film was evidently also released (in 2005) by the same label.

SPOOKIES (p.41) – Ad-line: *"They Want Your Blood!"* Formerly (*circa* late '80s) available on domestic VHS from Sony Video and also released on VHS in the UK by Palace Video. More recently it has been released on British PAL Region 2 DVD by VIPCO (Video Instant Picture Company) as part of that label's "Screamtime Collection" (*"Films That Terrified Audiences Around The World!"*). There is a more than watchable rip of the Brit vid version on YouTube, plus a couple trailers and numerous clips too.

100

ZOMBIE (p.60) – First released on domestic VHS in 1981 by Wizard Video—in their notorious "worm-face zombie" big box edition which is now so highly prized by collectors—the film was subsequently (1989) issued in the same tape format in the US by Magnum Entertainment. Anchor Bay Entertainment released it on both DVD and VHS in 1998, but their transfer print was unfortunately excessively grainy. A superior quality edition of the film was issued on domestic NTSC Region 1 DVD by Blue Underground (at 2.35:1) in 2004. It is currently available as an Amazon insta-vid in both HD and SD quality modes, priced accordingly for rental/purchase. In 2011, BU also issued it on Blu-ray in a "2-Disc Ultimate Edition", loaded with extras. Special featurettes for that release include: *Zombie Wasteland* (interviews with stars Ian McCulloch, Richard Johnson and Al Cliver, as well as actor/stuntman Ottaviano Dell'Acqua); *Flesh Eaters on Film* (an interview with co-producer Fabrizio de Angelis); *Deadtime Stories* (interviews with cowriters Elisa Briganti and Dardano Sacchetti); *World of the Dead* (interviews with DP Sergio Salvati and production/costume designer Walter Patriarca); *Zombi Italiano* (interviews with special makeup FX artists Giannetto De Rossi and Maurizio Trani and SFX artist Gino De Rossi); *Notes on a Headstone* (an interview with the film score's composer Fabio Frizzi); *All in the Family* (an interview with Antonella Fulci, Lucio's daughter); and *'Zombie' Lover* (in which Guillermo del Toro talks about the film, a favorite of his). There is also an audio commentary track with star Ian McCulloch and Jason J. Slater, editor of *Diabolik* magazine. According to BU's hype for this special edition: *"Each flesh-eating frame has been lovingly restored to skull-rotting perfection... Now fully-loaded with hours of brand new Extras, this is the Ultimate Edition of ZOMBIE!"*

French VHS

Printed in Great Britain
by Amazon